Quality Costs

201
Q&A

SAP Certified Application Associate
PLM-QM

ALSO BY BILLIE G. NORDMEYER

CALIBRATION INSPECTION
201 Q&A
SAP CERTIFIED APPLICATION ASSOCIATE PLM-QM

CATALOGS & INSPECTION METHODS
201 Q&A
SAP CERTIFIED APPLICATION ASSOCIATE PLM-QM

DEFECTS RECORDING
201 Q&A
SAP CERTIFIED APPLICATION ASSOCIATE PLM-QM

DYNAMIC MODIFICATION
201 Q&A
SAP CERTIFIED APPLICATION ASSOCIATE PLM-QM

INSPECTIION LOT COMPLETION
201 Q&A
SAP CERTIFIED APPLICATION ASSOCIATE PLM-QM

SAMPLE DETERMINATION
201 Q&A
SAP CERTIFIED APPLICATION ASSOCIATE PLM-QM

STABILITY STUDIES
201 Q&A
SAP CERTIFIED APPLICATION ASSOCIATE PLM-QM

TEST EQUIPMENT MANAGEMENT
201 Q&A
SAP CERTIFIED APPLICATION ASSOCIATE PLM-QM

Quality Costs

201
Q&A

SAP Certified Application Associate
PLM-QM

Billie G. Nordmeyer, MBA, MA

Library of Congress Cataloging in Publication Data has been applied for.

ISBN 13: 978-1503191310
ISBN 10: 1503191311

ABOUT THE AUTHOR

Billie G. Nordmeyer, MBA, MA is an SAP consultant, trainer and published author. She has held Senior Consultant and Business Development Manager of SAP Practice positions with a "Big 4" consulting firm, three "Fortune 100" firms and six "Fortune Most Admired Companies." Nordmeyer has consulted with Fortune 100 and Fortune 500 enterprises and supported clients in the aerospace, oil and gas, software, retail, pharmaceutical and manufacturing industries. Nordmeyer holds a BSBA in accounting, an MBA in finance and an MA in international management.

CONTENTS

INTRODUCTION

A technical certification is a valuable achievement in part because employers consider it confirmation that a job candidate is a well-qualified professional. Accordingly, if your goal is a position with a consulting firm, a major firm in industry or a leading not-for-profit organization, SAP certification training will help you get there. SAP training aimed at enhancing your understanding of particular concepts so you might sit for a standardized exam and obtain a professional credential is available both online and at bricks-and mortar institutions. But some training programs fail to accomplish the key objective...namely, prepare a candidate to achieve a passing grade on a certification exam.

In an exam setting, you must identify correct answers to questions that may bear little resemblance to the way major concepts are presented in the day-to-day operation of SAP applications. Consequently, while in your professional life you may play a key role in support of SAP software and solutions, to do well on the exam, you'll need training that provides a global view of interrelated functions and activities. But some training programs fail to provide a certification candidate either the information needed to perform well during a testing process or the means necessary to identify his training needs.

You should also be aware that SAP certification exams assume that, as a certification candidate, you're knowledgeable about definitions and master data, as well as the application of a fairly extensive set of transactions and customizing functions. For example, during the testing process, you may be expected to recognize specific attributes of major transactions and customizing functions, definitions of key system elements, the interrelationship among all of these factors, or other characteristics of the system to which you may not be exposed on a daily basis. Your training program, however, may fail to provide a sufficient number of questions and explanations for you to learn or confirm your knowledge of even the most perfunctory concepts addressed by the certification exam.

What's more, when sitting for the certification exam and the answer to each question is one of several different -- and often complex -- alternatives, you want to be assured ahead of time that you can make the right choice. Reviewing documentation or working through a relatively small number of practice test questions, however, may not provide you with the practical skills needed to apply your knowledge in a multiple-choice testing environment.

Hence this book series for the SAP Certified Application Consultant PLM-QM exam that allows you to enhance and test your knowledge using hundreds of multiple-choice questions well before you take the actual exam. The 201 Q&A SAP Certified Application Consultant PLM-QM book series is composed of individual books, each of which addresses one module, scenario or master data that may be covered in the certification exam. In turn, each study guide, such as Calibration Inspections, provides both a short and detailed answer for each of the 201 questions included in the book. These explanations allow you to grasp the bigger picture, connect new information with prior knowledge and use this knowledge to increase your score on the actual exam.

In the case that you want to review and analyze your knowledge pertaining to only one topic, you can purchase the one book that addresses that topic. If instead, you want to review a number of topics the exam may address, you can purchase some or all of the books in the series. In either case, using the 201 practice exam questions provided in each book, you can analyze your training needs in regards to one function, scenario or master data and then focus your study on the specific areas where you need to enhance your knowledge. In either case, I wish you the best of luck on the exam!

CHAPTER I

QUESTIONS

QUESTIONS

Q-01: Which of the following refers to actual costs that are incurred due to inspection and testing activities aimed at ensuring the consistent quality of a product and its conformance to established benchmarks?

A. Appraisal costs

B. Prevention costs

C. Nonconformity costs

Short Answer: 103
Answer & Explanation: 123

Q-02: Standard values must be defined for activity types to confirm activities for inspection operations. Where are the values defined?

A. CO component

B. PP component

C. QM component

Short Answer: 103
Answer & Explanation: 123

Q-03:   Which of the following is a prerequisite to the confirmation of activities for an inspection operation? Select all that apply.

A. Create activity types

B. Create standard values for activity times

C. Create cost centers

D. Create order categories

E. Create machine times

Short Answer: 103
Answer & Explanation: 125

Q-04:   How do you ensure that appraisal costs are assigned to a cost center? Select all that apply.

A. Select the special settlement rule in QM order

B. Select the standard settlement receiver control indicator in QM order

C. Set the individual QM order control indicator in material master record inspection setup

Short Answer: 103
Answer & Explanation: 127

Q-05:   In what circumstance is a general QM order for appraisal costs used? Select all that apply.

A. The need exists to use a single order to collect appraisal costs for a number of materials

B. The need does not exist to assign the accumulated costs to particular materials

C. The need exists to settle the accumulated costs on an as incurred basis

D. The need exists to use an automatic function to create the order on an ad hoc basis

Short Answer: 103
Answer & Explanation: 128

Q-06:   Which of the following is a step that is required to process an individual QM order for appraisal costs in the QM component? Select all that apply.

A. Create the QM order when the inspection lot is created

B. Assign the inspection lot or material to the QM order

C. Record inspection results

D. Confirm activities for the inspection operation

E. Enter usage decision for inspection lot

Short Answer: 103

Answer & Explanation: 129

Q-07: How is the account assignment object determined for nonconformity costs that are incurred due to the poor quality of materials.

A. Order type is assigned to the account assignment object

B. Notification type is assigned to the account assignment object

C. Notification type is assigned to the QM order type

Short Answer: 103
Answer & Explanation: 131

Q-08: A QM order for inspection costs is assigned to a material. What customer requirement is met by doing so? Select all that apply.

A. Collect costs on short-term basis

B. Settle costs on a periodic basis

C. Create QM order automatically

Short Answer: 103
Answer & Explanation: 132

Q-09: A material number is a selection criteria for what QM order report?

A. QM order by inspection type report

B. Cost report for QM order

C. Cost report for inspection lot

Short Answer: 103
Answer & Explanation: 133

Q-10:   In what case is the standard settlement receiver used in the creation and assignment of a new QM order?

A. Costs should be settled to a CO internal order on a one-time basis

B. Costs should be settled to more than one CO internal order on a periodic basis

C. Costs should be settled to a cost center on a one-time basis

D. Costs should be settled to more than one Controlling internal order on a one-time basis

Short Answer: 104
Answer & Explanation: 134

Q-11:   Which of the following determines the QM order type that is used to collect appraisal costs for a single inspection lot?

A. QM order type defined in Customizing

B. QM order type specified for the inspection type in the material master record

C. Create QM Order function

Short Answer: 104
Answer & Explanation: 136

Q-12:   What step in the production process triggers the entry of nonconformity costs? Select all that apply.

A. Completion of a defect analysis or a corrective action

B. Completion of a quality notification

C. Creation of a defect record

D. Creation of a quality notification

E. Completion of a quality inspection

Short Answer: 104
Answer & Explanation: 137

Q-13:   Labor costs have been incorrectly allocated to a particular cost center following an inspection. What should be checked? Select all that apply.

A. Activity types defined for the work center

B. Assignment of work center to cost center

C. Prices defined for activity types

Short Answer: 104
Answer & Explanation: 138

Q-14: Expenses incurred during an inspection are allocated to a cost object on a one-time basis regardless of the time at which the appraisal costs are incurred. This process is referred to as _____?

A. Long-term cost settlement

B. Periodic cost settlement

C. One-time cost settlement

Short Answer: 104
Answer & Explanation: 140

Q-15: Labor costs related to an inspection are not confirmed for an individual inspection lot. What change may need to be made?

A. Specify order type for inspection type

B. Specify order type for material type

C. Specify order type for plant

Short Answer: 104
Answer & Explanation: 141

Q-16: What is required to ensure that the confirmation of activities for a specific QM order is mandatory?

A. Work center confirmation indicator for operation control key

B. Milestone confirmation indicator for operation control key

C. Labor confirmation indicator for operation control key

Short Answer: 104
Answer & Explanation: 143

Q-17: On what basis does the inspection type determine that a particular QM order type should be created?

A. Order category is assigned to the inspection type in the material master record

B. Order type is assigned to the order category in the material master record

C. Order type is assigned to the inspection type in the material master record

Short Answer: 104
Answer & Explanation: 143

Q-18:   Which of the following refers to costs that are incurred due to the failure of the characteristics of a material to conform to material specifications or a prescribed standard? Select all that apply.

A. Appraisal costs

B. Prevention costs

C. Nonconformity costs

Short Answer: 104
Answer & Explanation: 145

Q-19:   What function can be used to record activity times that are accounted for by a general QM order for appraisal costs? Select all that apply.

A. Central Maintenance

B. Results Recording

C. Usage Decision

D. Defects Recording

Short Answer: 104
Answer & Explanation: 145

Q-20:   The customer wants to use the general QM order to manage appraisal costs. What requirement is met by doing so?

A. Accumulate appraisal costs for multiple materials using one order

B. Accumulate appraisal costs for one material using multiple orders

C. Accumulate appraisal costs for multiple materials using multiple orders

D. Accumulate appraisal costs for one material using one order

Short Answer: 104
Answer & Explanation: 147

Q-21: What customer requirement is met by the assignment of the general QM order type to the inspection type in the material master record?

A. Order will be a short-term cost collector

B. Multiple inspection lots will be assigned to the QM order

C. Goods movements will be posted with account assignments

Short Answer: 104
Answer & Explanation: 148

Q-22: How would you view summarized costs for multiple inspection lots?

A. Display QM orders by inspection type

B. Display cost report for QM order

C. Display cost report for inspection lot confirmed activities

Short Answer: 104
Answer & Explanation: 149

Q-23:   Which of the following is a required entry when the Central Maintenance function is used to create and assign a QM order? Select all that apply.

A. Plant

B. Inspection type

C. Material

D. Order type

Short Answer: 104
Answer & Explanation: 149

Q-24:   What data is documented in the Display of QM Orders by Inspection Type? Select all that apply.

A. Material number

B. Order type

C. Inspection type

D. Activity times

E. Plant

Short Answer: 105
Answer & Explanation: 150

Q-25:   On what basis are the actual costs of an
inspection determined? Select all that apply.

A. Activity times

B. Inspection type

C. Activity prices

D. Cost center

E. Production order

Short Answer: 105
Answer & Explanation: 150

Q-26:   Which of the following is a required entry for
the confirmation of activities using the Results
Recording function? Select all that apply.

A. Work center

B. Setup Time

C. Plant

D. Labor

E. Machine time

Short Answer: 105
Answer & Explanation: 152

Q-27:   Your customer wants to determine the ways in
which the organization might become more productive
by decreasing the number of products that are returned
and by reducing the amount of work performed if a
product is returned. Which of the following might be
used by the customer to make this evaluation?

A. Preventive costs

B. Appraisal costs

C. Nonconformity costs

Short Answer: 105
Answer & Explanation: 153

Q-28:   The customer wants to record QM costs that
arise from the lack of conformance of a product to a
specification. What types of costs might these be?
Select all that apply.

A. Material costs

B. Rework costs

C. Training costs

D. Warranty costs

Short Answer: 105
Answer & Explanation: 154

Q-29:   What setting is needed to classify cost-related orders that originate in the QM component?

A. Order category

B. Order type

C. Activity type

Short Answer: 105
Answer & Explanation: 154

Q-30:   How is the actual cost of a QM inspection determined? Select all that apply.

A. Order type

B. Inspection type

C. Order category

D. Activity types

E. Activity times

Short Answer: 105
Answer & Explanation: 155

Q-31:   Which of the following is a valid QM Quality Costs function? Select all that apply.

A. Create QM order

B. Assign activity type

C. Replace QM order

D. Confirm activities

Short Answer: 105
Answer & Explanation: 156

Q-32:   How can the customer differentiate between the cost incurred to ensure the consistent quality of a product and the cost incurred due to the failure of a product to conform to its specifications?

A. Order category

B. Order type

C. Activity type

D. Activity category

Short Answer: 105
Answer & Explanation: 157

Q-33:   Why are quality inspection functions integrated with the Controlling component? Select all that apply.

A. Link QM order to account assignment object

B. Link activity type and activity time to cost
assignment object

C. Link order category to cost assignment object

Short Answer: 105
Answer & Explanation: 157

Q-34:   Which of the following refers to quality costs
for which activities are documented using the
Notifications component?

A. Prevention costs

B. Appraisal costs

C. Nonconformity costs

Short Answer: 105
Answer & Explanation: 158

Q-35:   What does nonconformity costs mean?

A. Costs incurred to prevent nonconformities of
products

B. Costs incurred to identify nonconformities of
products

C. Costs incurred to correct nonconformities of
products

Short Answer: 105

Answer & Explanation: 159

Q-36: Which of the following is considered when management reviews QM appraisal costs? Select all that apply.

A. Inspector training

B. Material used in an inspection

C. Defects costs

D. Test equipment

Short Answer: 105
Answer & Explanation: 159

Q-37: How are warranty expenses classified in the Quality Management component?

A. Appraisal costs

B. Nonconformity costs

Short Answer: 105
Answer & Explanation: 160

Q-38: What statement is true regarding an individual QM order for appraisal costs? Select all that apply.

A. Long-term cost collector

B. Short-term cost collector

C. Collects costs for one material or one inspection lot to which it is assigned

D. Collects costs for more than one material or inspection lot

Short Answer: 106
Answer & Explanation: 160

Q-39:   What is the purpose of the QM order type?

A. Differentiate order according to its functional origin

B. Link QM order to Controlling component

C. Determine parameters that control how the order is processed

Short Answer: 106
Answer & Explanation: 161

Q-40:   How does the system determine that QM quality costs are to be assigned to an individual material or inspection lot?

A. QM order type QL01

B. QM order type QL02

C. QM order type QN01

Short Answer: 106
Answer & Explanation: 163

Q-41: The customer has decided that the costs that are incurred due to the poor quality of materials should be collected on a cost center basis. What setting is required to accomplish this objective? Select all that apply.

A. Assign order type to the notification type

B. Assign order category to the notification type

C. Assign account assignment object to the order category

D. Assign account assignment object to the order type

E. Assign account assignment object to the notification type

Short Answer: 106
Answer & Explanation: 164

Q-42: What leads to the generation of the QM order for nonconformity costs?

A. Results Recording function used to document a critical defect for future processing

B. Usage Decision function used to document a critical defect for future processing

C. Change Notification function

Short Answer: 106
Answer & Explanation: 165

Q-43:   The special settlement rule control indicator is selected during the creation of a new QM order. What requirement is met by doing so?

A. Settlement of costs to a single cost center or CO internal order

B. Settlement of costs to multiple receivers or an account assignment object according to a distribution rule

Short Answer: 106
Answer & Explanation: 166

Q-44:   A customer wants to settle inspection costs to several receivers. How is this achieved?

A. Special settlement rule control indicator is selected during the creation of the order

B. Standard settlement rule control indicator is selected during the creation of the order

Short Answer: 106
Answer & Explanation: 166

Q-45:   True or False. A benefit of the use of an individual QM order for appraisal costs versus a general

QM order for appraisal costs is the ability to trace appraisal costs to an individual material or inspection lot.

A. True

B. False

Short Answer: 106
Answer & Explanation: 167

Q-46: What Quality Management function can be used to confirm activities for an inspection operation? Select all that apply.

A. Results Recording

B. Inspection Lot Completion

C. Usage Decision

Short Answer: 106
Answer & Explanation: 167

Q-47: When is an individual QM order type required for the confirmation of activities for inspection operations?

A. Collect costs for multiple inspection lots

B. Assign appraisal costs to individual material

C. Collect appraisal costs on a short-term basis

Short Answer: 106
Answer & Explanation: 168

Q-48:   Where is the milestone confirmation control indicator selected for the confirmation of activities during the results recording process?

A. Inspection operation in QM Customizing application

B. Inspection characteristic in QM Customizing application

C. Task list header

Short Answer: 106
Answer & Explanation: 170

Q-49:   You want to make the entry of inspection activities to be mandatory. What setting is required to do so?

A. "Milestone confirmation" control indicator for operation control key

B. "Milestone confirmation" control indicator for characteristic control key

C. "Milestone confirmation" control indicator for task list control key

Short Answer: 107
Answer & Explanation: 170

Q-50:   Which of the following is true regarding the QM order for appraisal costs order types? Select all that apply.

A. Order is cost collector for one or more materials or inspection lots

B. Order is short-term or long-term cost collector

C. Order is created with manual or automatic process

Short Answer: 107
Answer & Explanation: 171

Q-51:   Which of the following is used to record appraisal costs? Select all that apply.

A. Labor costs

B. Rework costs

C. Material costs

D. Warranty costs

Short Answer: 107
Answer & Explanation: 172

Q-52:   The customer wants to view QM orders related to a particular plant. What report will allow the customer to do so?

A. Cost report for QM order

B. QM orders by inspection type report

C. Cost report for confirmed activities for an inspection lot

Short Answer: 107
Answer & Explanation: 172

Q-53:   The customer wants to define a unique QM order type for the collection of nonconformity costs that are incurred as a quality notification is processed. Is this possible?

A. Yes

B. No

Short Answer: 107
Answer & Explanation: 173

Q-54:   How would you account for appraisal costs that are incurred for more than one inspection lot? Select all that apply.

A. General QM order

B. Individual QM order

C. QM order for nonconformity costs

Short Answer: 107

Answer & Explanation: 174

Q-55:   In what circumstance should an individual QM order for appraisal costs be used? Select all that apply.

A. The need does not exist to collect costs for a number of materials

B. The need exists to assign the accumulated costs to particular materials or inspection lots

C. The need exists to settle the accumulated costs on a periodic basis

D. The need exists to use a manual function to create the QM order

Short Answer: 107
Answer & Explanation: 175

Q-56:   The QM order list by inspection type is used for what reason?

A. Costs for individual inspection lot

B. List of orders for a specific material, plant and/or inspection type

C. Summarized costs for inspection lots or materials

Short Answer: 107
Answer & Explanation: 176

Q-57:   T/F   A benefit of the use of an individual QM order for appraisal costs versus a general QM order for appraisal costs is the ability to trace appraisal costs to an individual material or inspection lot.

A. True

B. False

Short Answer: 107
Answer & Explanation: 176

Q-58:   What is a prerequisite to the creation and assignment of a new QM order for the single settlement of quality costs? Select all that apply.

A. Activity type

B. Material master record

C. Cost center

D. Activity price

E. Account assignment object

Short Answer: 107
Answer & Explanation: 177

Q-59:   Activity times are converted by the Controlling component to costs on the basis of_____?

A. Activity type

B. Activity type price

C. Cost element

Short Answer: 107
Answer & Explanation: 178

Q-60:   For what reason do inspection activities require activity types and prices?

A. Activity confirmation for inspection type

B. Activity confirmation for production order

C. Activity confirmation for inspection operation

Short Answer: 107
Answer & Explanation: 180

Q-61:   Why is the standard settlement receiver control indicator or the specific settlement rule control indicator required during the creation of a new QM order?

A. Determines the material assignment for the QM order

B. Determines the account assignment for the QM order

C. Determines the plant assignment for the QM order

Short Answer: 108
Answer & Explanation: 181

Q-62:   In what case does a QM order refer to more than one cost center or CO internal order?

A. Standard settlement receiver control indicator is selected in the QM order

B. Special settlement rule control indicator is selected in the QM order

Short Answer: 108
Answer & Explanation: 182

Q-63:   What conditions must be met to confirm activities for an inspection operation? Select all that apply.

A. Assign work center to inspection plan operation in PP

B. Assign QM order to inspection lot

C. Define prices in CO

D. Define activity types in QM

Short Answer: 108
Answer & Explanation: 183

Q-64:   What option is available to confirm activities for an inspection operation? Select all that apply.

A. Defects Recording function

B. Results Recording function

C. Usage Decision function

Short Answer: 108
Answer & Explanation: 184

Q-65:   How does the customer differentiate appraisal costs for one inspection operation from another?

A. Work center

B. Inspection type

C. Material number

Short Answer: 108
Answer & Explanation: 185

Q-66:   What function can be used to record setup time and labor time incurred during the inspection of a material? Select all that apply.

A. Results Recording

B. Usage Decision

C. Defects Recording

D. Inspection Lot Completion

Short Answer: 108

Answer & Explanation: 186

Q-67: Which of the following is an activity type that is defined for a quality inspection? Select all that apply.

A. Material

B. Rework

C. Labor

Short Answer: 108
Answer & Explanation: 187

Q-68: Automatic creation of order and short-term cost collector are characteristics of which of the following?

A. Individual QM order for appraisal costs

B. General QM order for appraisal costs

C. QM order for nonconformity costs

Short Answer: 108
Answer & Explanation: 187

Q-69: What functions exist to display and evaluate cost data that is associated with QM orders? Select all that apply.

A. QM orders by inspection type

B. Cost report for confirmed activities for inspection type

C. Cost report by cost center

D. QM orders by inspection lot

Short Answer: 108
Answer & Explanation: 188

Q-70:   Which of the following is a type of nonconformity cost? Select all that apply.

A. Labor costs

B. Rework costs

C. Material costs

D. Warranty costs

Short Answer: 108
Answer & Explanation: 188

Q-71:   What solution automatically calculates the actual costs of a QM inspection?

A. Quality Management

B. Controlling

C. Finance

Short Answer: 108
Answer & Explanation: 189

Q-72:   What is unique about the general QM Order for appraisal costs? Select all that apply.

A. No account assignment

B. Account assignment

C. Long-term cost collector

D. Short- term cost collector

Short Answer: 108
Answer & Explanation: 190

Q-73:   Why is the QM Results Recording function integrated with the Controlling component?

A. Enable the settlement of appraisal costs that are confirmed in the form of activity times on the QM order

B. Enable the settlement of nonconformity costs that are confirmed in the form of activity times on the QM order

C. Enable the settlement of preventive costs that are confirmed in the form of activity times on the QM order

Short Answer: 108

Answer & Explanation: 190

Q-74: The customer requires the ability to assign QM appraisal costs for more than one material or inspection lot to a QM order. What order type should be used?

A. QL01

B. QL02

C. QN01

Short Answer: 109
Answer & Explanation: 191

Q-75: Which of the following is a reason that an individual QM order for appraisal costs should be selected rather than the general QM order for appraisal costs? Select all that apply.

A. The customer requires a short-term cost collector

B. The customer requires the ability to collect costs on an individual inspection lot basis

C. The customer requires the ability to collect costs on an individual inspection type basis

D. The customer requires the ability to settle costs on a periodic basis

Short Answer: 109

Answer & Explanation: 192

Q-76:   What function is used to account for
nonconformity costs that are incurred while processing
a quality notification?

A. Change General QM Order

B. Change QM Order for Nonconformity Costs

C. Change Quality Notification

Short Answer: 109
Answer & Explanation: 193

Q-77:   What is recorded in the Quality Management
system to support the calculation of the actual appraisal
costs that are incurred to process an inspection lot?
Select all that apply.

A. Activity types

B. Prices

C. Activity times

Short Answer: 109
Answer & Explanation: 194

Q-78:   Identify a valid QM order type.

A. General QM order for nonconformity costs

B. Individual QM order for appraisal costs

C. QM order for appraisal costs

Short Answer: 109
Answer & Explanation: 195

Q-79:   Which of the following requires an account assignment to record costs as an inspection lot is processed?

A. Individual QM order

B. General QM order

Short Answer: 109
Answer & Explanation: 195

Q-80:   What criteria are used to select quality management data during the creation of a QM order for a single inspection lot? Select all that apply.

A. Plant

B. Material

C. WBS element

D. Order type

Short Answer: 109
Answer & Explanation: 196

Q-81: What assignments must be made to confirm activities for an inspection operation? Select all that apply.

A. Assignment of work center to cost center in PP

B. Assignment of activity type to work center in PP

C. Assignment of work center to operation in inspection plan in QM

Short Answer: 109
Answer & Explanation: 197

Q-82: Which of the following functions is performed by the CO component, rather than the QM component, as an inspection lot is processed? Select all that apply.

A. Creation of the QM order for the management of the appraisal costs

B. Entry of the activity times in the QM order

C. Settlement of the actual costs for the QM order

Short Answer: 109
Answer & Explanation: 198

Q-83: What Controlling component data is integrated with the Quality Management component for purposes of managing quality-related costs?

48

A. Work center

B. Activity type values

C. Activity types

Short Answer: 109
Answer & Explanation: 199

Q-84:   The costs associated with the inspection of a
material are not accurately reflected in the cost center.
What might be the issue? Select all that apply.

A. Incorrect work center entered when inspection
   results are recorded

B. Incorrect plant entered when inspection results are
   recorded

C. Incorrect milestone confirmed

D. Incorrect controlling area entered when inspection
   results are recorded

E. Incorrect cost center entered when inspection
   results are recorded

Short Answer: 109
Answer & Explanation: 199

Q-85:   Which of the following is not a required step
to confirm inspection activities during the results
recording process?

A. Enter set-up time

B. Enter work center

C. Enter labor time

Short Answer: 109
Answer & Explanation: 200

Q-86:   How would you ensure that you can create a QM order on the basis of multiple inspection types?

A. Class selection function in the Create QM Order function

B. Plant selection function in the Create QM Order function

C. Multiple selection function in the Create QM Order function

Short Answer: 110
Answer & Explanation: 201

Q-87:   Identify a purpose of the cost report for a general QM order?

A. Summarize costs for all materials or inspection lots associated with an individual QM order for quality costs

B. Summarize costs for all materials or inspection lots associated with a general order for appraisal costs

C. Summarize costs for all materials or inspection lots associated with an individual QM order for nonconformity costs

Short Answer: 110
Answer & Explanation: 202

Q-88:   How would you describe QM quality costs? Select all that apply.

A. Costs incurred to prevent quality issues

B. Costs incurred to inspect the quality of a product or material

C. Costs incurred due to the failure to maintain acceptable quality levels

Short Answer: 110
Answer & Explanation: 203

Q-89:   Identify an attribute of a QM order for nonconformity costs.

A. Order is created with automatic procedures

B. Account assignment for the order is specified

C. Costs for the order are settled in the Notifications component

Short Answer: 110
Answer & Explanation: 204

Q-90:   How can the customer differentiate an appraisal cost from a nonconformity cost?

A. Order category

B. Order type

C. Activity type

Short Answer: 110
Answer & Explanation: 205

Q-91:   Which of the following is the QM order type that is used to accumulate nonconformity costs?

A. QL01

B. QL02

C. QN03

Short Answer: 110
Answer & Explanation: 205

Q-92:   What considerations point to the use of a general QM order for appraisal costs? Select all that apply.

A. The customer requires that an order type be a long-term cost collector

B. The customer requires the ability to accumulate and segregate the costs for a single material

C. The customer requires the ability to settle costs on a monthly basis

D. The customer requires the ability to record nonconformity costs without an account assignment

Short Answer: 110
Answer & Explanation: 206

Q-93: How would you record appraisal costs in a way that ensures visibility to the material and inspection lot to which the costs originated?

A. QM order type QL01

B. QM order type QL02

C. QM order type QN01

Short Answer: 110
Answer & Explanation: 207

Q-94: Inspection costs for a particular material have not been settled to the appropriate cost center. What may be the issue? Select all that apply.

A. Incorrect settlement receiver is entered in QM order

B. Incorrect special settlement rule is entered in QM order

C. Incorrect plant is entered in QM order

D. Incorrect material is entered in QM order

Short Answer: 110
Answer & Explanation: 208

Q-95:   Which of the following is a valid function
related to the collection of costs incurred during quality
inspections? Select all that apply.

A. Create QM Order

B. Display QM Order by Material

C. Delete QM Order

Short Answer: 110
Answer & Explanation: 209

Q-96:   When a QM order is created for an individual
inspection lot, on what basis can the activity data be
selected? Select all that apply.

A. Plant

B. Material

C. Inspection lot

D. Activity type

E. Material class

Short Answer: 110
Answer & Explanation: 210

Q-97: What criteria can be used to record the actual costs incurred during a quality inspection when an individual cost center is used for the single settlement of costs? Select all that apply.

A. Client

B. Inspection type

C. Material class

D. Material type

Short Answer: 111
Answer & Explanation: 211

Q-98: The customer wants to confirm activities for inspection operations while recording inspection results. What is a QM requirement to do so?

A. Assign order to work center

B. Define activity types

C. Assign work center to operation in plan

D. Define activity type prices

E. Define standard values for activity types in operation

Short Answer: 111
Answer & Explanation: 212

Q-99:   On what basis is the Production Planning component integrated with the Quality Management component for purposes of capturing quality-related costs?

A. Order is assigned to work center

B. Activity types are defined for each work center

C. Standard values are defined for cost center

Short Answer: 111
Answer & Explanation: 214

Q-100:   The customer wants the system to automatically display a dialog box for the confirmation of activities during the results recording process. What Customizing setting is required to do so?

A. Confirmation required control indicator for the QM order

B. Confirmation required control indicator for the inspection type

C. Confirmation required control indicator for the inspection operation

Short Answer: 111

Answer & Explanation: 215

Q-101: What alternative is available to view QM orders?

A. QM order by inspection type

B. QM order by plant

C. QM order by material class

Short Answer: 111
Answer & Explanation: 217

Q-102: The dollars to be charged to a cost center or other cost accumulator for a particular activity type is defined in the Controlling component whereas the activity types are defined in the _____component.

A. Controlling

B. Quality Management

C. Production Planning

Short Answer: 111
Answer & Explanation: 218

Q-103: How does the system determine the work center for which the activity times should be confirmed?

A. Work center assigned to inspection type

B. Work center assigned to inspection characteristic

C. Work center assigned to inspection operation

Short Answer: 111
Answer & Explanation: 219

Q-104: On what basis are the actual costs of the quality inspection of a single inspection lot determined?

A. Activity type

B. Cost center

C. Date

Short Answer: 111
Answer & Explanation: 220

Q-105: How would you access the cost elements, activity times and confirmed costs for a general QM order?

A. Display QM orders by inspection type

B. Display cost report for QM order

C. Display cost report for inspection lot confirmed activities

Short Answer: 111
Answer & Explanation: 221

Q-106: Which of the following occurs when a quality notification is processed?

A. Costs incurred to prevent quality issues are recorded

B. Costs incurred to inspect the quality of a product or material are recorded

C. Costs incurred due to the failure to maintain an acceptable quality level of a product or material are recorded

Short Answer: 111
Answer & Explanation: 222

Q-107: What does the Quality Notification component use to collect costs that arise due to the poor quality of a material? Select all that apply.

A. Order category 08

B. Order category 06

C. Order type QL01

D. Order type QL02

E. Order type QN01

Short Answer: 111
Answer & Explanation: 222

Q-108: How would you access the summarized costs for all materials assigned to a particular QM order?

A. Confirmed activities for inspection lot cost report

B. Cost report for QM order

C. QM orders by inspection type

Short Answer: 111
Answer & Explanation: 223

Q-109: What is required to enable the automatic collection of activity times that lead to the determination of the actual costs incurred for a particular inspection lot? Select all that apply.

A. Assignment of QM order to an inspection lot

B. Creation of a general QM order

C. Selection of the milestone confirmation control indicator in the material master record

Short Answer: 111
Answer & Explanation: 224

Q-110: Which of the following is controlled by the general QM appraisal costs order type? Select all that apply.

A. The term for which the order collects inspection costs

B. The materials for which the order collects inspection costs

C. The inspection lots for which the order collects inspection costs

D. The functions used to confirm the activities for an inspection operation to the QM order

Short Answer: 112
Answer & Explanation: 225

Q-111: What leads to the automatic creation of an individual QM order for appraisal costs?

A. QL01

B. QL02

C. QL03

Short Answer: 112
Answer & Explanation: 227

Q-112: Where is the setting made that associates a particular QM order to a specific quality inspection?

A. Material master record

B. Inspection lot

C. Inspection type

Short Answer: 112
Answer & Explanation: 227

Q-113: What is the purpose of a controlling area and cost center or CO internal order in relation to a QM order?

A. Settlement rule

B. Periodic settlement of costs

C. Cost settlement receiver

D. Account assignment of QM order

Short Answer: 112
Answer & Explanation: 229

Q-114: How would you access the summarized costs for all inspection lots associated with a particular QM order?

A. QM order by inspection type

B. Cost report for a QM order

C. Cost report for confirmed activities for inspection lot

Short Answer: 112
Answer & Explanation: 230

Q-115: What criteria are used to record the actual costs incurred during a quality inspection using a CO internal order? Select all that apply.

A. Plant

B. Inspection type

C. Client

D. Material type

Short Answer: 112
Answer & Explanation: 231

Q-116: What criteria are used to record the actual costs incurred during a quality inspection for more than one cost center? Select all that apply.

A. Plant

B. Client

C. Internal order

D. Material type

Short Answer: 112
Answer & Explanation: 231

Q-117: What is controlled by the class selection function when creating and assigning a general QM order?

A. Selection of a material from a material class to which the QM order will be assigned

B. Selection of a QM order for which a material class is created

C. Selection of a cost center for which a QM order is created

D. Selection of a controlling area for which a CO internal order is created

Short Answer: 112
Answer & Explanation: 232

Q-118:   Why is the work center significant in the confirmation of activities for a quality inspection?

A. Work center is assigned to cost center

B. Work center is assigned to QM order

C. Work center is assigned to inspection operation

Short Answer: 112
Answer & Explanation: 233

Q-119:   How would you display cost data for an individual QM order?

A. QM order by inspection type report

B. Cost report for QM order

C. Cost report confirmed activities for inspection lot

Short Answer: 112
Answer & Explanation: 234

Q-120:   Labor costs related to an inspection are not confirmed. What change may need to be made? Select all that apply.

A. Define activity types in CO

B. Assign work center to cost center in PM

C. Assign work center to inspection plan operation in PP

Short Answer: 112
Answer & Explanation: 235

Q-121:   An organization fails to maintain a desired quality level. Which of the following are examples of QM costs that are incurred as a result of this failure? Select all that apply.

A. Defect costs

B. Material costs

C. Inspector training costs

D. Warranty costs

65

Short Answer: 112
Answer & Explanation: 236

Q-122:   How would you display a cost report for a general QM order type that summarizes costs for all materials related to the order?

A. QM orders by inspection type

B. Cost report for QM order

C. Cost report for confirmed activities for an inspection lot

Short Answer: 112
Answer & Explanation: 236

Q-123:   You want to confirm activities for an inspection operation as you enter a usage decision for the inspection lot. What is required to do so? Select all that apply.

A. Define prices for activity types

B. Assign work centers to inspection plan characteristics

C. Assign QM order to inspection lot

Short Answer: 112
Answer & Explanation: 237

Q-124: The activity types and prices that are required to confirm activities for inspection operations are defined where?

A. QM component

B. PP component

C. CO component

Short Answer: 113
Answer & Explanation: 238

Q-125: How are quality costs associated with work centers?

A. Activity types maintained according to work center

B. Work center is assigned to cost center

C. Work center is assigned to inspection operation

Short Answer: 113
Answer & Explanation: 239

Q-126: What QM settings ensure that appraisal costs are assigned to a cost center?

A. Work center is assigned to inspection operation

B. Work center is assigned to cost center

C. Work center is assigned to activity types

Short Answer: 113
Answer & Explanation: 241

Q-127: An incorrect work center is proposed when a confirmation of activities for an operation is performed? What could be the issue?

A. Incorrect work center is assigned to the cost center

B. Incorrect work center is proposed from last confirmation

C. Incorrect work center is assigned to inspection plan operation

Short Answer: 113
Answer & Explanation: 242

Q-128: A customer wants to settle inspection costs to one cost center. How is this achieved?

A. Standard settlement receiver control indicator is selected in the QM order

B. Special settlement rule control indicator is selected in the QM order

Short Answer: 113
Answer & Explanation: 243

Q-129: How would you access a summary of costs that originate with the inspection lots assigned to a QM order?

A. QM orders by inspection type

B. Cost report for QM order

C. Cost report for confirmed activities for an inspection lot

Short Answer: 113
Answer & Explanation: 244

Q-130:   You want to confirm activities for a QM order during the results recording processes. What entries are required to do so? Select all that apply.

A. Milestone confirmation key

B. Set-up time

C. Work center

D. Plant

E. Labor

Short Answer: 113
Answer & Explanation: 245

Q-131:   When a QM order is created, a general QM order type, rather than an individual QM order type, is used. What is the result of this error?

A. The same result as if the individual QM order was selected.

B. Costs appear too high in that the order collects costs for more than one material or lot

C. Costs are assigned to a material and then allocated to the inspection lot

D. Costs cannot be assigned to an individual material

Short Answer: 113
Answer & Explanation: 245

Q-132: When the customer records activity times incurred during a QM quality inspection, what occurs? Select all that apply.

A. The QM component identifies the predefined prices associated with the activity types for which the activity times were recorded in the CO component

B. The CO component converts the activity times to actual costs on the basis of the predefined prices stored in the CO component

C. The CO component identifies the predefined prices associated with the activity types for which the activity times were recorded in the QM component

D. The QM component converts the activity times to actual costs on the basis of the predefined prices stored in the CO component

Short Answer: 113

Q-133:   In what circumstance is an individual QM order for appraisal costs used? Select all that apply.

A. The need exists to collect costs for a number of materials

B. The need exists to assign inspection costs to a particular material or product

C. The need exists to settle the accumulated costs on a periodic basis

D. The need exists to use an automatic function to create the order on an ad hoc basis

Short Answer: 113
Answer & Explanation: 247

Q-134:   How would you access a list of QM orders that were created on the basis of a particular material and plant?

A. Display QM orders by inspection type

B. Display cost report for QM order

C. Display cost report for inspection lot confirmed activities

Short Answer: 114
Answer & Explanation: 248

Q-135: What step leads to the creation of a QM order for the collection of appraisal costs for an individual inspection lot?

A. Creation of inspection lot

B. Creation of notification

C. Completion of inspection lot

Short Answer: 114
Answer & Explanation: 249

Q-136: What does "standard settlement receiver" mean in relation to a QM order?

A. Complete settlement of costs will occur using a cost center or CO internal order on a one-time basis

B. Settlement of costs will occur using multiple receivers or an account assignment object on a periodic basis

Short Answer: 114
Answer & Explanation: 250

Q-137: What criteria influence the creation of an individual QM order for an inspection lot? Select all that apply.

A. Company code

B. Plant

C. Inspection lot

D. Inspection type

E. Material class

Short Answer: 114
Answer & Explanation: 252

Q-138:   How is the settlement of appraisal costs to a
cost center controlled when an individual QM order for
appraisal costs is created?

A. Standard settlement receiver control indicator in the
   order

B. Special settlement rule control indicator in the order

C. Cost center multiple selection function

Short Answer: 114
Answer & Explanation: 253

Q-139:   A new QM order is created. However, activity
costs are applied to an incorrect cost center. Why?

A. Incorrect cost center assigned to work center

B. Incorrect controlling area assigned to work center

C. Incorrect settlement rule assigned to work center

Short Answer: 114

Q-140:   The assignment of a work center to an inspection plan operation is required to confirm activities for inspection operations. In what component is this assignment made?

A. CO

B. PP

C. QM

Short Answer: 114
Answer & Explanation: 256

Q-141:   What sequence of tasks is required to confirm activities for an inspection operation?

A. CO activities, PP activities, QM activities

B. PP activities, CO activities, QM activities

C. QM activities, PP activities, CO activities

Short Answer: 114
Answer & Explanation: 257

Q-142:   The dollars to be charged to a cost center or the cost accumulator for a particular activity type is defined where?

A. Production Planning

B. Quality Management

C. Controlling

Short Answer: 114
Answer & Explanation: 258

Q-143:   How is the cost center determined as activities are confirmed for an inspection operation?

A. Work center is assigned to operation in plan in QM

B. Work center is assigned to cost center in PP

C. Work center is defined for activity types in operation

Short Answer: 114
Answer & Explanation: 259

Q-144:   Which of the following describes an activity type? Select all that apply.

A. Used for external activity allocations

B. Represented by units of measure including labor hours

C. Represents a group of resources in a cost center

Short Answer: 114
Answer & Explanation: 261

Q-145: Which of the following is required to account for nonconformity costs? Select all that apply.

A. Quality notification

B. Quality notification type

C. Quality Management order type QL01

D. Quality Management order category 05

E. Account assignment object

Short Answer: 115
Answer & Explanation: 261

Q-146: Which of the following is documented as quality-related costs using the QM component? Select all that apply.

A. Prevention costs

B. Appraisal costs

C. Nonconformity costs

Short Answer: 115
Answer & Explanation: 262

Q-147: How would you account for appraisal costs incurred for a single inspection lot? 7
A. General QM order

B. Individual QM order

C. QM order for nonconformity costs

Short Answer: 115
Answer & Explanation: 263

Q-148:   The inspection lot is completed. However, the appraisal costs cannot be traced to the material. Why might this occur?

A. Order type QL01 was used to create the QM order as a cost collector

B. Order type QL02 was used to create the QM order as a cost collector

C. Order type QL03 was used to create the QM order as a cost collector

Short Answer: 115
Answer & Explanation: 263

Q-149:   For what reason does the Controlling component search for a price that is associated with a particular activity type, which represents a task that is performed at a work center during a quality inspection?

A. The CO component uses the price to convert activity times recorded for activity types in QM to actual costs of the activities performed

B. The CO component uses the price to convert activity times recorded for activity types in CO to actual costs of the activity performed

C. The QM component uses the price to convert activity times recorded for activity types in QM to actual costs of the activities performed

D. The QM component uses the price to convert activity times recorded for activity types in CO to actual costs of the activity performed

Short Answer: 115
Answer & Explanation: 265

Q-150:   What application component automatically creates an order type QN01 when a critical defect is documented?

A. Notifications

B. Inspection Lot Completion

C. Results Recording

D. Any of the above

E. None of the above

Short Answer: 115
Answer & Explanation: 265

Q-151: What is assigned to the material master record to document appraisal costs? Select all that apply.

A. QM order type

B. Activity type

C. Order category

Short Answer: 115
Answer & Explanation: 266

Q-152: What is the purpose of the order type QL02?

A. Post goods movement with account assignment

B. Post goods movement without account assignment

C. Post goods movement with account assignment to cost center

D. Post goods movement to warehouse stock

Short Answer: 115
Answer & Explanation: 267

Q-153: What controls the settlement of costs to multiple receivers according to a distribution rule?

A. Standard settlement receiver control indicator

B. Special settlement rule control indicator

Short Answer: 115
Answer & Explanation: 267

Q-154: A QM order is not assigned to an inspection lot during a production inspection? Why?

A. Production order is used as a cost collector for the production inspection type

B. QM is not active for the inspected material
C. Standard inspection types are not used for the production orders

Short Answer: 115
Answer & Explanation: 268

Q-155: Why is the assignment of a work center to a cost center mandatory to account for quality-related costs?

A. Create QM order

B. Confirm activities for inspection operations

C. Settlement of costs

Short Answer: 115
Answer & Explanation: 269

Q-156: The system creates a quality notification. Which of the following statements is true?

A. Appraisal costs will be recorded

B. Nonconformity costs will be recorded

C. Preventive costs will be recorded

Short Answer: 115
Answer & Explanation: 269

Q-157:   Which Controlling element is used to classify a cost order that originates in the QM application?

A. Order category 06

B. Order category 08

C. Order category 09

Short Answer: 116
Answer & Explanation: 270

Q-158:   Which of the following enables the assignment of multiple materials to the QM order but precludes the assignment of costs to individual materials?

A. General QM order for appraisal costs

B. Individual QM order for appraisal costs

C. QM order for nonconformity costs

Short Answer: 116
Answer & Explanation: 271

Q-159: What function is used to confirm activities for inspection operations? Select all that apply.

A. Defects Recording

B. Results Recording

C. Usage Decision

Short Answer: 116
Answer & Explanation: 271

Q-160: Why is an individual QM order assigned to an inspection lot?

A. Collect appraisal costs for a material

B. Collect appraisal costs for an inspection operation

C. Collect appraisal costs for an inspection type

Short Answer: 116
Answer & Explanation: 272

Q-161: T/F It is possible to create a QM order that does not assign costs to either a material or an inspection lot.

A. True

B. False

Short Answer: 116

Answer & Explanation: 273

Q-162:   What is a difference between one individual
QM order for appraisal costs and another? Select all
that apply.

A. Order type

B. Account assignment object for inspection lot

C. Assignment of inspection lot to order

Short Answer: 116
Answer & Explanation: 274

Q-163:   Inspection type, QM order and material are
examples of what?

A. Selection criteria for creation of cost report for QM
   order

B. Selection criteria for creation of QM orders by
   inspection type list

C. Selection criteria for creation of cost report for
   confirmed activities for an inspection lot

Short Answer: 116
Answer & Explanation: 275

Q-164:   What must occur in Production Planning to
confirm inspection operation activities?

A. Definition of activity types

B. Assignment of work center to cost center

C. Definition of standard values for activity types

Short Answer: 116
Answer & Explanation: 275

Q-165: The confirmation of activities during results recording is done in reference to what object?

A. Inspection operation

B. Inspection characteristic

C. Inspection lot

Short Answer: 116
Answer & Explanation: 276

Q-166: What are the benefits of recording QM quality-related costs? Select all that apply.

A. Identify the costs of poor quality

B. Take actions to control appraisal costs that represent rework and warranty expense

C. Improve productivity

D. Take action to control defects that lead to appraisal costs

Short Answer: 116
Answer & Explanation: 277

Q-167:   Which solution automatically records warranty expenses?

A. Inspection Lot Processing

B. Inspection Lot Completion

C. Quality Notifications

D. Controlling

Short Answer: 116
Answer & Explanation: 277

Q-168:   What options are available to process QM inspection costs? Select all that apply.

A. QM order for appraisal costs for one inspection lot

B. QM order for appraisal costs for more than one inspection lot

C. QM order for nonconformity costs for one inspection lot

D. QM order for nonconformity costs for more than one inspection lot

Short Answer: 116
Answer & Explanation: 278

Q-169: Under what circumstance is the central maintenance function used to create a QM order? Select all that apply.

A. Create general QM order for appraisal costs

B. Create individual QM order for appraisal costs

C. Create QM order for nonconformity costs

Short Answer: 116
Answer & Explanation: 279

Q-170: You want to create an order to collect inspection costs for a specific inspection lot. How does the system determine the type of order to be created?

A. QM order type determined by material master record inspection type setting

B. Order category determined by material master record inspection type settings

C. QM order type determined by customer enhancement

D. QM order type determined by plant level settings

E. Settlement rule determined by plant level settings

Short Answer: 117
Answer & Explanation: 279

Q-171: Which of the following is a true statement regarding quality-related costs? Select all that apply.

A. Settlement rules are defined in the QM order master records

B. WBS element and profit segment are examples of receivers defined in the distribution rule

C. Distribution rule determines how costs are settled

D. Cost element used to settle quality costs defined in settlement rule in the material master record

Short Answer: 117
Answer & Explanation: 280

Q-172: What transaction is used to create a QM order for nonconformity costs? Select all that apply.

A. Change Quality Notification

B. Results Recording

C. Usage Decision

Short Answer: 117
Answer & Explanation: 281

Q-173: You want to assign nonconformity costs to the appropriate object. How does the system determine the object to which the costs are assigned?

A. QM order is assigned to the quality notification

B. QM order is assigned to the material master record

C. QM order is assigned to the inspection lot

Short Answer: 117
Answer & Explanation: 282

Q-174: How is the settlement of costs to multiple receivers planned when a QM order is created?

A. Distribution rule

B. Class selection rule

C. Special settlement rule

D. Standard settlement receiver

Short Answer: 117
Answer & Explanation: 283

Q-175: How is the settlement of costs to a CO internal order controlled?

A. Distribution rule

B. Class selection rule

C. Standard settlement receiver

D. Special settlement rule

Short Answer: 117
Answer & Explanation: 285

Q-176:   A new QM order is created. However, the costs were settled to only one receiver. Why?

A. Special settlement rule is selected

B. Standard settlement rule is selected

C. Class selection rule is selected

Short Answer: 117
Answer & Explanation: 286

Q-177:   The wrong value is recorded for appraisal costs. What should be checked? Select all that apply.

A. Activity type prices defined in CO

B. Activity types defined for work center in QM

C. Assignment of work center to inspection plan operation in QM

D. All of the above

E. None of the above

Short Answer: 117
Answer & Explanation: 287

Q-178: What must be available to collect nonconformity costs in the Controlling component? Select all that apply.

A. Controlling account assignment object

B. QM order type

C. Controlling order category

D. All of the above

E. None of the above

Short Answer: 117
Answer & Explanation: 288

Q-179: Definition of standard values for activity types, assignment of work center to cost center and creation of activity types are examples of what?

A. Prerequisites to the creation and assignment of a QM order using the central maintenance function

B. Prerequisites to the confirmation of activities for an inspection operation

C. Prerequisites to the creation and assignment of a QM order using a manual process

Short Answer: 117
Answer & Explanation: 289

Q-180: The documentation of labor costs for a quality inspection requires which of the following? Select all that apply.

A. Setup time

B. Machine time

C. Labor time

D. Work center

E. Plant

Short Answer: 117
Answer & Explanation: 290

Q-181: Which of the following is a valid QM order type?

A. Custom QM order type

B. Individual QM order for nonconformity costs

C. General QM order for nonconformity costs

D. Individual QM order for appraisal costs

Short Answer: 117
Answer & Explanation: 291

Q-182: Activities are recorded on a labor, machine time, and setup time basis. What requirement is met by doing so?

A. Document costs that originate with inspection activities

B. Document costs that originate with notification activities

Short Answer: 118
Answer & Explanation: 292

Q-183: The customer wants to use the central maintenance function to create and assign QM appraisal orders to materials. What selection criterion must be entered during the process?

A. Inspection type

B. Plant

C. Material

Short Answer: 118
Answer & Explanation: 292

Q-184: The customer wants to record costs that are incurred due to quality inspection activities. What types of costs might these be? Select all that apply.

A. Material costs

B. Warranty costs

C. Labor costs

D. Equipment costs

E. Rework costs

Short Answer: 118
Answer & Explanation: 293

Q-185:   You create a QM order type QN01 for what purpose?

A. Collect costs that arise due to the poor quality of goods

B. Collect costs that arise due to the inspection of a material

C. Collect costs that arise due to the inspection of more than one material

Short Answer: 118
Answer & Explanation: 293

Q-186:   What statement is true regarding a general QM order for appraisal costs? Select all that apply.

A. Long-term cost collector

B. Short-term cost collector

C. Cost collector for one material or one inspection lot to which it is assigned

D. Cost collector for more than one material or inspection lot

Short Answer: 118
Answer & Explanation: 294

Q-187: Confirmed activity times for an order are converted to costs in the _____

component.

A. PP

B. QM

C. CO

Short Answer: 118
Answer & Explanation: 295

Q-188: Which of the following QM order types requires an account assignment? Select all that apply.

A. QL01

B. QL02

C. QN01

Short Answer: 118
Answer & Explanation: 296

Q-189:   Which of the following is a property of the QM order for nonconformity costs? Select all that apply.

A. Order is assigned to the notification header

B. The costs for the order are settled in the Controlling component

C. An account assignment for the order is not be specified

D. The order is created when the defect record is processed

Short Answer: 118
Answer & Explanation: 297

Q-190:   Which of the following can be specified for the settlement of costs using a QM order that is created to collect inspection costs for a single inspection lot? Select all that apply.

A. Cost center

B. CO internal order

C. Profit segment

D. Asset

Short Answer: 118
Answer & Explanation: 298

Q-191: The customer wants to collect appraisal costs on the basis of a particular cost center and assign a QM order to a material master. What function is used to achieve these objectives? Select all that apply.

A. Maintain Material Master Record

B. Maintain QM Order

C. Central Maintenance

Short Answer: 118
Answer & Explanation: 299

Q-192: The customer has decided he wants to settle inspection costs for an inspection lot of the basis of an account assignment object and a distribution rule. Where are the controls set?

A. QM order

B. Material master record

C. Account assignment object

Short Answer: 118
Answer & Explanation: 299

Q–193: Which of the following is a circumstance in which the user foregoes the use of an individual QM order for appraisal costs and instead selects the general QM order for appraisal costs? Select all that apply.

A. The need does not exist to collect costs for a
   number of materials

B. The need does exist to assign the accumulated costs
   to a particular material or inspection lot

C. The need does exist to settle the accumulated costs
   on an as incurred basis

D. The need does exist to use an automatic function to
   create the order

Short Answer: 118
Answer & Explanation: 300

Q-194: The standard settlement receiver control
indicator is selected during the creation of a new QM
order. What requirement is met by doing so?

A. Settlement of costs to a single cost center or CO
   internal order

B. Settlement of costs to multiple receivers or an
   account assignment object on the basis of a
   distribution rule

Short Answer: 119
Answer & Explanation: 301

Q-195: When a quality notification is completed,
nonconformity costs are not settled to a cost object.
Which of the following reflects the possible impact of
this omission? Select all that apply.

A. Defect costs will be overstated

B. Rework costs will be understated

C. Inspector training costs will be overstated

D. Warranty costs will be understated

Short Answer: 119
Answer & Explanation: 302

Q-196:   Which of the following is used by the system to determine the QM order type that will be used to document appraisal costs for one material when an inspection lot is created?

A. Inspection settings in material master record

B. Account assignment settings

C. Settlement rule

Short Answer: 119
Answer & Explanation: 303

Q-197:   Which of the following activities are required to post QM appraisal costs in the Controlling component?

A. Assign work center to cost center

B. Create activity types for cost center

C. Define standard values for inspection characteristics

Short Answer: 119
Answer & Explanation: 304

Q-198:   What QM function can be used to confirm activities for inspection operations? Select all that apply.

A. Results Recording

B. Defects Recording

C. Usage Decision

Short Answer: 119
Answer & Explanation: 304

Q-199:   What does "confirmation required" mean in relation to the Results Recording function?

A. Activity times must be recorded for a QM order

B. Activity prices must be recorded for a QM order

C. Activity types must be recorded for a QM order

Short Answer: 119
Answer & Explanation: 305

Q-200:   Erroneous inspection costs have been allocated to a cost center. What should be checked? Select all that apply.

A. Activity types defined for activity types in CO

B. Assignment of work center to cost center in PP

C. Prices defined for activity types in CO

Short Answer: 119
Answer & Explanation: 306

Q-201:   The customer wants quality costs to be settled
to multiple receivers or an account assignment object.
What settlement rule is selected to accomplish this
objective?

A. Special settlement receiver

B. Standard settlement receiver

Short Answer: 119
Answer & Explanation: 307

CHAPTER II

SHORT ANSWERS

SHORT ANSWERS

Q-01:   A. Appraisal costs

Q-02:   A. CO component

Q-03:   A. Create activity types and C. Create cost centers

Q-04:   B. Select the standard settlement receiver control indicator in QM order

Q-05:   A. The need exists to use a single order to collect appraisal costs for a number of materials and B. The need does not exist to assign the accumulated costs to particular materials

Q-06:   A. Create the QM order when the inspection lot is created, B. Assign the inspection lot or material to the QM order and D. Confirm activities for the inspection operation

Q-07:   C. Notification type is assigned to the QM order type

Q-08:   A. Collect costs on short-term basis and C. Create QM order automatically

Q-09:   A. QM order by inspection type

Q-10:   A. Costs should be settled to a CO internal order on a one-time basis and C. Costs should be settled to a cost center on a one-time basis

Q-11:   C. Create QM Order function

Q-12:   B. Completion of a quality notification

Q-13:   B. Assignment of work center to cost center

Q-14:   C. One-time cost settlement

Q-15:   A. Specify order type for inspection type

Q-16:   B. Milestone confirmation indicator for operation control key

Q-17:   C. Order type is assigned to the inspection type in the material master record

Q-18:   C. Nonconformity costs

Q-19:   B. Results Recording and C. Usage Decision

Q-20:   A. Accumulate appraisal costs for multiple materials using one order

Q-21:   B. Multiple inspection lots will be assigned to the QM order

Q-22:   B. Display cost report for QM order

Q-23:   A. Plant and D. Order type

Q-24:   A. Material number and C. Inspection type

Q-25:   A. Activity times and C. Activity prices

Q-26:   A. Work center and C. Plant

Q-27:   C. Nonconformity costs

Q-28:   B. Rework costs and D. Warranty costs

Q-29:   A. Order category

Q-30:   D. Activity types and E. Activity times

Q-31:   A. Create QM order, C. Replace QM order and D. Confirm activities

Q-32:   B. Order type

Q-33:   A. Link QM order to account assignment object

Q-34:   C. Nonconformity costs

Q-35:   C. Costs incurred to correct nonconformities of products

Q-36:   B. Material used in an inspection and D. Test equipment

Q-37:   B. Nonconformity costs

Q-38:   B. Short-term cost collector and C. Collects costs for one material or one inspection lot to which it is assigned

Q-39:   C. Determine parameters that control how the order is processed

Q-40:   B. QM order type QL02

Q-41:   A. Assign order type to the notification type and D. Assign account assignment object to the order type

Q-42:   C. Change Notification function

Q-43:   B. Settlement of costs to multiple receivers or an account assignment object according to a distribution rule

Q-44:   A. Special settlement rule control indicator is selected during the creation of the order

Q-45:   A. True

Q-46:   A. Results Recording and C. Usage Decision

Q-47:   B. Assign appraisal costs to individual material and C. Collect appraisal costs on short-term basis

Q-48:   A. Inspection operation in QM Customizing application

Q-49:   A. "Milestone confirmation" control indicator
         for operation control key

Q-50:   A. Order is cost collector for one or more
         materials or inspection lots and B. Order is
         short-term or long-term cost collector

Q-51:   A. Labor costs and C. Material costs

Q-52:   B. QM orders by inspection type report

Q-53:   A. Yes

Q-54:   A. General QM order

Q-55:   A. The need does not exist to collect costs for
         a number of materials and B. The need exists
         to assign the accumulated costs to particular
         materials or inspection lots

Q-56:   B. List of orders for a specific material, plant
         and/or inspection type

Q-57:   A. True

Q-58:   A. Activity type and D. Activity price

Q-59:   B. Activity type price

Q-60:   C. Activity confirmation for inspection
         operation

Q-61: B. Determines the account assignment for the QM order

Q-62: B. Special settlement rule control indicator is selected in the QM order

Q-63: B. Assign QM order to inspection lot and C. Define prices in CO

Q-64: B. Results Recording function and C. Usage Decision function

Q-65: A. Work center

Q-66: A. Results Recording and B. Usage Decision

Q-67: A. Material and C. Labor

Q-68: A. Individual QM order for appraisal costs

Q-69: A. QM orders by inspection type

Q-70: B. Rework costs and D. Warranty costs

Q-71: B. Controlling

Q-72: A. No account assignment and C. Long-term cost collector

Q-73: A. Enable the settlement of appraisal costs that are confirmed in the form of activity times on the QM order

Q-74:   A. QL01

Q-75:   A. The customer requires a short-term cost collector and B. The customer requires the ability to collect costs on an individual inspection lot basis

Q-76:   C. Change Quality Notification

Q-77:   A. Activity types and C. Activity times

Q-78:   B. Individual QM order for appraisal costs

Q-79:   A. Individual QM order

Q-80:   A. Plant and B. Material

Q-81:   A. Assignment of work center to cost center in PP and C. Assignment of work center to operation in inspection plan in QM

Q-82:   C. Settlement of the actual costs for the QM order

Q-83:   C. Activity types

Q-84:   A. Incorrect work center entered when inspection results are recorded and B. Incorrect plant entered when inspection results are recorded

Q-85:   A. Enter set-up time and C. Enter labor time

Q-86: C. Multiple selection function in Create QM Order function

Q-87: B. Summarize costs for all materials or inspection lots associated with a general order for appraisal costs

Q-88: B. Costs incurred to inspect the quality of a product or material and C. Costs incurred due to the failure to maintain acceptable quality levels

Q-89: B. Account assignment for the order is specified

Q-90: B. Order type

Q-91: C. QN03

Q-92: A. The customer requires that the order type be a long-term cost collector and C. The customer requires the ability to settle costs on a monthly basis

Q-93: B. QM order type QL02

Q-94: A. Incorrect settlement receiver is entered in QM order

Q-95: A. Create QM Order

Q-96: A. Plant and B. Material

Q-97:   B. Inspection type and C. Material class

Q-98:   C. Assign work center to operation in plan and E. Define standard values for activity types in operation

Q-99:   B. Activity types are defined for each work center

Q-100:   C. Confirmation required control indicator for the inspection operation

Q-101:   A. QM order by inspection type

Q-102:   A. Controlling

Q-103:   C. Work center assigned to inspection operation

Q-104:   A. Activity type

Q-105:   B. Display cost report for QM order

Q-106:   D. Costs incurred due to the failure to maintain an acceptable quality level of a product or material are recorded

Q-107:   B. Order category 06 and E. Order type QN01

Q-108:   B. Cost report for QM order

Q-109:   A. Assignment of QM order to an inspection lot

Q-110: A. The term for which the order collects inspection costs

Q-111: B. QL02

Q-112: A. Material master record

Q-113: C. Cost settlement receiver

Q-114: B. Cost report for a QM order

Q-115: A. Plant and B. Inspection type

Q-116: A. Plant

Q-117: B. Selection of a material from a material class to which the QM order will be assigned

Q-118: A. Work center is assigned to cost center and C. Work center is assigned to inspection operation

Q-119: B. Cost report for QM order

Q-120: A. Define activity types in CO

Q-121: A. Defect costs and D. Warranty costs

Q-122: B. Cost report for QM order

Q-123: A. Define prices for activity types and C. Assign QM order to inspection lot

Q-124: C. CO component

Q-125: B. Work center is assigned to cost center and C. Work center is assigned to inspection operation

Q-126: A. Work center is assigned to inspection operation

Q-127: C. Incorrect work center is assigned to inspection plan operation

Q-128: A. Standard settlement receiver control indicator is selected in the QM order

Q-129: B. Cost report for QM order

Q-130: C. Work center and D. Plant

Q-131: D. Costs cannot be assigned to an individual material

Q-132: B. The CO component converts the activity times to actual costs on the basis of the predefined prices stored in the CO component and C. The CO component identifies the predefined prices associated with the activity types for which the activity times were recorded in the QM component

Q-133: B. The need exists to assign inspection costs to a particular material or product and D. The need exists to use an automatic function to create the order on an ad hoc basis

Q-134: A. Display QM orders by inspection type

Q-135: A. Creation of inspection lot

Q-136: A. Complete settlement of costs will occur using a cost center or CO internal order on a one-time basis

Q-137: B. Plant, D. Inspection type and E. Material class

Q-138: A. Standard settlement receiver control indicator in the order

Q-139: A. Incorrect cost center assigned to work center

Q-140: C. QM

Q-141: A. CO activities, PP activities and QM activities

Q-142: C. Controlling

Q-143: B. Work center is assigned to cost center in PP

Q-144: B. Represented by units of measure including labor hours and C. Represents a group of resources in a cost center

Q-145: A. Quality notification, B. Quality notification type and E. Account assignment object

Q-146: B. Appraisal costs and C. Nonconformity costs

Q-147: B. Individual QM order

Q-148: A. Order type QL01 was used to create the QM order as a cost collector

Q-149: A. The CO component uses the price to convert activity times recorded for activity types in QM to actual costs for the activities performed

Q-150: E. None of the above

Q-151: A. QM order type

Q-152: A. Post goods movement with account assignment and C. Post goods movement with account assignment to cost center

Q-153: B. Special settlement rule control indicator

Q-154: A. Production order is used as a cost collector for the production inspection type

Q-155: B. Confirm activities for inspection operations

Q-156: B. Nonconformity costs will be recorded

Q-157: A. Order category 06

Q-158: A. General QM order for appraisal costs

Q-159: B. Results Recording and C. Usage Decision

Q-160: A. Collect appraisal costs for a material

Q-161: A. True

Q-162: B. Account assignment object for inspection lot

Q-163: B. Selection criteria for creation of QM orders by inspection type list

Q-164: B. Assignment of work center to cost center

Q-165: A. Inspection operation

Q-166: A. Identify the costs of poor quality and C. Improve productivity

Q-167: D. Controlling

Q-168: A. QM order for appraisal costs for one inspection lot and B. QM order for appraisal costs for more than one inspection lot

Q-169: A. Create general QM order for appraisal costs and B. Create individual QM order for appraisal costs

Q-170:   A. QM order type determined by material master record inspection- type setting, C. QM order type determined by customer enhancement and D. QM order type determined by plant level setting

Q-171:   A. Settlement rules are defined in QM order master records and C. Distribution rule determines how costs are settled

Q-172:   A. Change Quality Notification

Q-173:   A. QM order is assigned to the quality notification

Q-174:   C. Special settlement rule

Q-175:   C. Standard settlement receiver

Q-176:   B. Standard settlement rule is selected

Q-177:   D. All of the above

Q-178:   D. All of the above

Q-179:   B. Prerequisites to the confirmation of activities for an inspection operation

Q-180:   D. Work center and E. Plant

Q-181:   A. Custom QM order type and D. Individual QM order for appraisal costs

Q-182:   A. Document costs that originate with
         inspection activities

Q-183:   B. Plant

Q-184:   A. Material costs, C. Labor costs and D.
         Equipment costs

Q-185:   A. Collect costs that arise due to the poor
         quality of goods

Q-186:   A. Long-term cost collector and D. Cost
         collector for more than one material or
         inspection lot

Q-187:   C. CO

Q-188:   B. QL02 and C. QN01

Q-189:   A. Order is assigned to the notification
         header and B. The costs for the order are
         settled in the Controlling component

Q-190:   A. Cost center and B. CO internal order

Q-191:   A. Maintain Material Master Record and C.
         Central Maintenance

Q-192:   A. QM order

Q-193:   C. The need does exist to settle the
         accumulated costs on an as incurred basis and

D. The need does exist to use an automatic function to create the order

Q-194:   A. Settlement of costs to a single cost center or CO internal order

Q-195:   B. Rework costs will be understated and D. Warranty costs will be understated

Q-196:   A. Inspection settings in material master record

Q-197:   A. Assign work center to cost center

Q-198:   A. Results Recording and C. Usage Decision

Q-199:   A. Activity times must be recorded for a QM order

Q-200:   B. Assignment of work center to cost center in PP and C. Prices defined for activity types in CO

Q-201:   A. Special settlement receiver

CHAPTER III

ANSWERS & EXPLANATIONS

ANSWERS & EXPLANATIONS

Q-01:   A. Appraisal costs

Efforts made to assure the quality of a product or service result in quality costs. The functions of the Quality Management component lead to the incurrence of two types of quality costs: appraisal costs and nonconformity costs. Nonconformity costs result from the creation of a product or service, the characteristics of which do not conform to defined specifications or standards. Such costs include defect costs, rework costs and warranty costs. In turn, appraisal costs result from the performance of inspections that confirm the quality of products and the conformance of the products to established benchmarks. Such costs include labor, material and equipment costs.

Q-02:   A. CO component

The Controlling component uses orders to plan, monitor and settle operating costs. QM orders are the means by which the activities that are performed during a quality inspection are linked to account assignment objects in the Controlling component. Like all costs accounted for by the Controlling component, an order category classifies the appraisal costs according to the functional origin of the costs. The functional origin of QM quality costs is indicated by the order category 06. In turn, standard QM order for appraisal costs order types or custom order types are used to collect the costs

that originate with inspection activities. The type of QM order used can be determined by the assignment of an order type to the material master record inspection type in Customizing. For example, the general QM order for appraisal costs is a long-term cost collector that's created with a manual process and used to collect costs for more than one inspection lot or material. These costs settled periodically. In turn, the individual QM order for appraisal costs is a short-term cost collector that's created automatically and used to collect inspection costs for a single inspection lot or material. These costs are settled on a one-time basis. To account for appraisal costs using an individual QM order for appraisal costs, the order is created as the inspection lot is created. The order is then assigned to the inspection lot. Following the inspection, inspection activities are recorded in the QM order in terms of activity types that are defined for a work center and related activity times as characteristic inspection results are recorded and valuated or as the usage decision for the inspection lot is documented. Next, the CO component retrieves predefined prices for the documented activity types and uses the prices to convert the activity times to actual costs. These appraisal costs are settled to a cost object, such as a cost center or a CO internal order, according to a settlement rule that's defined for the QM order master record. In turn, settlement profiles, which are defined in Customizing, determine the allowed receiver for each order type. When the appraisal costs are settled to cost objects, the system generates offsetting entries to the sender objects, whereas the debit postings remain in place. The confirmation of activities for quality inspection operations requires the creation of activity types for work centers and activity prices in Controlling and the assignment of work centers to cost objects in PP. Activity confirmation also requires the assignment of a work center to a plan operation, the definition of standard values for activity types and the assignment of the QM order to the inspection lot in QM. Also needed is the assignment of a QM order to the inspection lot and the use of an inspection plan for the inspection.

Q-03:   A. Create activity types and C. Create cost centers

The Controlling component uses orders to plan, monitor and settle operating costs. QM orders are the means by which the activities that are performed during a quality inspection are linked to account assignment objects in the Controlling component. Like all costs accounted for by the Controlling component, an order category classifies the appraisal costs according to the functional origin of the costs. The functional origin of QM quality costs is indicated by the order category 06. In turn, standard QM order for appraisal costs order types or custom order types are used to collect the costs that originate with inspection activities. The type of QM order used can be determined by the assignment of an order type to the material master record inspection type in Customizing. For example, the general QM order for appraisal costs is a long-term cost collector that's created with a manual process and used to collect costs for more than one inspection lot or material. These costs settled periodically. In turn, the individual QM order for appraisal costs is a short-term cost collector that's created automatically and used to collect inspection costs for a single inspection lot or material. These costs are settled on a one-time basis. To account for appraisal costs using an individual QM order for appraisal costs, the order is created as the inspection lot is created. The order is then assigned to the inspection lot. Following the inspection, inspection activities are recorded in the QM order in terms of activity types that are defined for a work center and related activity times as characteristic inspection results are recorded and valuated or as the usage decision for the inspection lot is documented. Next, the CO component retrieves predefined prices for the documented activity types and uses the prices to convert the activity times to actual costs. These appraisal costs are settled to a cost object, such as a cost center or a CO internal order, according to a settlement rule that's defined for the QM order master record. In turn, settlement profiles, which are defined in Customizing, determine the allowed receiver for each order type. When the appraisal costs are settled to cost objects, the system generates offsetting entries to the sender objects, whereas the debit postings remain in place. The confirmation of activities for quality inspection operations requires the creation of activity types for work centers and activity prices in Controlling and the assignment of work centers to cost objects in PP. Activity confirmation also requires the assignment of a work center to a plan operation, the definition of standard values for activity types and the assignment of the QM order to the inspection lot in QM. Also needed is the assignment of a QM order to the inspection lot and the use of an inspection plan for the inspection.

Q-04:   B. Select the standard settlement receiver
control indicator in QM order

The Controlling component uses orders to plan,
monitor and settle operating costs. QM orders are the
means by which the activities that are performed during
a quality inspection are linked to account assignment
objects in the Controlling component. Like all costs
accounted for by the Controlling component, an order
category classifies the appraisal costs according to the
functional origin of the costs. The functional origin of
QM quality costs is indicated by the order category 06.
In turn, standard QM order for appraisal costs order
types or custom order types are used to collect the costs
that originate with inspection activities. The type of
QM order used can be determined by the assignment of
an order type to the material master record inspection
type in Customizing. For example, the general QM
order for appraisal costs is a long-term cost collector
that's created with a manual process and used to collect
costs for more than one inspection lot or material.
These costs settled periodically. In turn, the individual
QM order for appraisal costs is a short-term cost
collector that's created automatically and used to collect
inspection costs for a single inspection lot or material.
These costs are settled on a one-time basis. To account
for appraisal costs using an individual QM order for
appraisal costs, the order is created as the inspection lot
is created. The order is then assigned to the inspection
lot. Following the inspection, inspection activities are
recorded in the QM order in terms of activity types that
are defined for a work center and related activity times
as characteristic inspection results are recorded and

valuated or as the usage decision for the inspection lot is documented. Next, the CO component retrieves predefined prices for the documented activity types and uses the prices to convert the activity times to actual costs. These appraisal costs are settled to a cost object, such as a cost center or a CO internal order, according to a settlement rule that's defined for the QM order master record. In turn, settlement profiles, which are defined in Customizing, determine the allowed receiver for each order type. When the appraisal costs are settled to cost objects, the system generates offsetting entries to the sender objects, whereas the debit postings remain in place. The confirmation of activities for quality inspection operations requires the creation of activity types for work centers and activity prices in Controlling and the assignment of work centers to cost objects in PP. Activity confirmation also requires the assignment of a work center to a plan operation, the definition of standard values for activity types and the assignment of the QM order to the inspection lot in QM. Also needed is the assignment of a QM order to the inspection lot and the use of an inspection plan for the inspection.

Q-05:   A. The need exists to use a single order to collect appraisal costs for a number of materials and B. The need does not exist to assign the accumulated costs to particular materials

The Controlling component uses orders to plan, monitor and settle operating costs. QM orders are the means by which the activities that are performed during a quality inspection are linked to cost assignment objects in the Controlling component. Like all costs accounted for by the Controlling component, an order category classifies the appraisal costs according to the functional origin of the costs. The functional origin of QM quality costs is indicated by the order category 06. In turn, standard QM order for appraisal costs order types or custom order types are used to collect the costs that originate with inspection activities. The type of QM order used can be determined by the assignment of an order type to the material master record inspection type in Customizing. For example, the general QM order for appraisal costs is a long-term cost collector that's created with a manual process and used to collect costs for more than one inspection lot or material. These costs are settled periodically. In turn, the individual QM order for appraisal costs is a short-term cost collector used to collect inspection costs for a single inspection lot or material. These costs are settled on a one-time basis.

Q-06:   A. Create the QM order when the inspection lot is created, B. Assign the inspection lot or material to the QM order and D. Confirm activities for the inspection operation

The Controlling component uses orders to plan, monitor and settle operating costs. QM orders are the means by which the activities that are performed during a quality inspection are linked to account assignment objects in the Controlling component. Like all costs accounted for by the Controlling component, an order category classifies the appraisal costs according to the functional origin of the costs. The functional origin of

QM quality costs is indicated by the order category 06. In turn, standard QM order for appraisal costs order types or custom order types are used to collect the costs that originate with inspection activities. The type of QM order used can be determined by the assignment of an order type to the material master record inspection type in Customizing. For example, the individual QM order for appraisal costs is a short-term cost collector that's created automatically and used to collect inspection costs for a single inspection lot or material. These costs are settled on a one-time basis. To account for appraisal costs using an individual QM order for appraisal costs, the order is created as the inspection lot is created. The order is then assigned to the inspection lot. Following the inspection, inspection activities are recorded in the QM order in terms of activity types that are defined for a work center and related activity times as characteristic inspection results are recorded and valuated or as the usage decision for the inspection lot is documented. Next, the CO component retrieves predefined prices for the documented activity types and uses the prices to convert the activity times to actual costs. These appraisal costs are settled to a cost object, such as a cost center or a CO internal order, according to a settlement rule that's defined for the QM order master record. In turn, settlement profiles, which are defined in Customizing, determine the allowed receiver for each order type. When the appraisal costs are settled to cost objects, the system generates offsetting entries to the sender objects, whereas the debit postings remain in place.

Q-07:   C. Notification type is assigned to the QM order type

The Controlling component uses orders to plan, monitor and settle operating costs. QM orders are the means by which the activities that are performed during a quality inspection are linked to account assignment objects in the Controlling component. Like all costs accounted for by the Controlling component, an order category classifies the appraisal costs according to the functional origin of the costs. The functional origin of QM quality costs is indicated by the order category 06. In turn, standard QM order for appraisal costs order types or custom order types are used to collect the costs that originate with inspection activities. The type of QM order used can be determined by the assignment of an order type to the material master record inspection type in Customizing. For example, the individual QM order for appraisal costs is a short-term cost collector that's created automatically and used to collect inspection costs for a single inspection lot or material. These costs are settled on a one-time basis. To account for appraisal costs using an individual QM order for appraisal costs, the order is created as the inspection lot is created. The order is then assigned to the inspection lot. Following the inspection, inspection activities are recorded in the QM order in terms of activity types that are defined for a work center and related activity times as characteristic inspection results are recorded and valuated or as the usage decision for the inspection lot is documented. Next, the CO component retrieves predefined prices for the documented activity types and uses the prices to convert the activity times to actual costs. These appraisal costs are settled to a cost object, such as a cost center or a CO internal order, according to a settlement rule that's defined for the QM order master record. In turn, settlement profiles, which are defined in Customizing, determine the allowed receiver for each order type. When the appraisal costs are settled to cost objects, the system generates offsetting entries to the sender objects, whereas the debit postings remain in place.

Q-08:   A. Collect costs on short-term basis and C. Create QM order automatically

The Controlling component uses orders to plan, monitor and settle operating costs. QM orders are the means by which the activities that are performed during a quality inspection are linked to account assignment objects in the Controlling component. Like all costs accounted for by the Controlling component, an order category classifies the appraisal costs according to the functional origin of the costs. The functional origin of QM quality costs is indicated by the order category 06. In turn, standard QM order for appraisal costs order types or custom order types are used to collect the costs that originate with inspection activities. The type of QM order used can be determined by the assignment of an order type to the material master record inspection type in Customizing. For example, the individual QM order for appraisal costs is a short-term cost collector that's created automatically and used to collect inspection costs for a single inspection lot or material. These costs are settled on a one-time basis. To account for appraisal costs using an individual QM order for appraisal costs, the order is created as the inspection lot is created. The order is then assigned to the inspection lot. Following the inspection, inspection activities are recorded in the QM order in terms of activity types that are defined for a work center and related activity times as characteristic inspection results are recorded and valuated or as the usage decision for the inspection lot is documented. Next, the CO component retrieves predefined prices for the documented activity types and uses the prices to convert the activity times to actual costs. These appraisal costs are settled to a cost object, such as a cost center or a CO internal order, according to a settlement rule that's defined for the QM order master record. In turn, settlement profiles, which are defined in Customizing, determine the allowed receiver for each order type. When the appraisal costs are settled to cost objects, the system generates offsetting entries to the sender objects, whereas the debit postings remain in place.

Q-09:   A. QM order by inspection type

The Controlling component uses orders to plan, monitor and settle operating costs. QM orders are the means by which the activities that are performed during quality inspections are linked to account assignment objects in the Controlling component. The documented appraisal costs data can be evaluated using three different Quality Costs functions: Display QM Orders by Inspection Type, Display Cost Report for QM Order and Display Cost Report for Inspection Lot Confirmed Activities. In particular, the QM Orders by Inspection Type List refers to all materials for which a QM order has been created that meet selection criteria, which include inspection type, material, plant and QM order. The list, which organizes the orders according to material number, includes the material short text, inspection type and inspection type description fields. After the list is created, the user can select an order and display the QM data that's documented in the related material master record or the related Controlling data.

Q-10:   A. Costs should be settled to a CO internal order on a one-time basis and C. Costs should be settled to a cost center on a one-time basis

The Controlling component uses orders to plan, monitor and settle operating costs. QM orders are the means by which the activities that are performed during a quality inspection are linked to account assignment objects in the Controlling component. Like all costs accounted for by the Controlling component, an order category classifies the appraisal costs according to the functional origin of the costs. The functional origin of QM quality costs is indicated by the order category 06. In turn, standard QM order for appraisal costs order types or custom order types are used to collect the costs that originate with inspection activities. The type of QM order used can be determined by the assignment of an order type to the material master record inspection type in Customizing. For example, the general QM order for appraisal costs is a long-term cost collector that's created with a manual process and used to collect costs for more than one inspection lot or material. These costs settled periodically. In turn, the individual QM order for appraisal costs is a short-term cost collector that's created automatically and used to collect inspection costs for a single inspection lot or material. These costs are settled on a one-time basis. To account for appraisal costs using an individual QM order for appraisal costs, the order is created as the inspection lot is created. The order is then assigned to the inspection lot. Following the inspection, inspection activities are recorded in the QM order in terms of activity types that are defined for a work center and related activity times as characteristic inspection results are recorded and valuated or as the usage decision for the inspection lot is documented. Next, the CO component retrieves predefined prices for the documented activity types and uses the prices to convert the activity times to actual costs. These appraisal costs are settled to a cost object, such as a cost center or a CO internal order, according to a settlement rule that's defined for the QM order master record. In turn, settlement profiles, which are defined in Customizing, determine the allowed receiver for each order type. When the appraisal costs are settled to cost objects, the system generates offsetting entries to the sender objects, whereas the debit postings remain in place. The confirmation of activities for quality inspection operations requires the creation of activity types for work centers and activity prices in Controlling and the assignment of work centers to cost objects in PP. Activity confirmation also requires the assignment of a work center to a plan operation, the definition of standard values for activity types and the assignment of the QM order to the inspection lot in QM. Also needed is the assignment of a QM order to the inspection lot and the use of an inspection plan for the inspection.

Q-11:   C. Create QM Order function

The Controlling component uses orders to plan, monitor and settle operating costs. QM orders are the means by which the activities that are performed during a quality inspection are linked to account assignment objects in the Controlling component. Like all costs accounted for by the Controlling component, an order category classifies the appraisal costs according to the functional origin of the costs. The functional origin of QM quality costs is indicated by the order category 06. In turn, standard QM order for appraisal costs order types or custom order types are used to collect the costs that originate with inspection activities. The type of QM order used can be determined by the assignment of an order type to the material master record inspection type in Customizing.   For example, the general QM order for appraisal costs is a long-term cost collector that's created with a manual process and used to collect costs for more than one inspection lot or material. These costs settled periodically. In turn, the individual QM order for appraisal costs is a short-term cost collector that's created automatically and used to collect inspection costs for a single inspection lot or material. These costs are settled on a one-time basis. To account for appraisal costs using an individual QM order for appraisal costs, the order is created as the inspection lot is created. The order is then assigned to the inspection lot. Following the inspection, inspection activities are recorded in the QM order in terms of activity types that are defined for a work center and related activity times as characteristic inspection results are recorded and valuated or as the usage decision for the inspection lot is documented. Next, the CO component retrieves predefined prices for the documented activity types and uses the prices to convert the activity times to actual costs. These appraisal costs are settled to a cost object, such as a cost center or a CO internal order, according to a settlement rule that's defined for the QM order master record. In turn, settlement profiles, which are defined in Customizing, determine the allowed receiver for each order type. When the appraisal costs are settled to cost objects, the system generates offsetting entries to the sender objects, whereas the debit postings remain in place.

Q-12:   B. Completion of a quality notification

The Controlling component uses orders to plan, monitor and settle operating costs. QM orders are the means by which activities that are performed to process a notification are linked to cost assignment objects in the Controlling component. As with all costs accounted for by the Controlling component, an order category is used to classify notification costs according to the functional origin of the costs. The order category for quality notifications is 06. In turn, a new or existing standard QM order for nonconformity costs is used to collect costs that originate with notification activities. The QM order type for notifications is QN01. To account for nonconformity costs using the QM order QN01, the order is created manually and assigned to the notification header as the notification is processed. As the notification is processed, the activities are recorded in the QM order in terms of activity types and activity times. The CO component then retrieves predefined prices for the documented activity types and uses the prices to convert the activity times to actual costs. These nonconformity costs that are incurred to process the notification are then settled to one or more cost objects, such as a cost center or a CO internal order, according to the account assignment that is entered when the QM order was created. When the nonconformity costs are settled to cost objects, the system automatically generates offsetting entries to the sender objects whereas the debit postings remain in place.

Q-13:   B. Assignment of work center to cost center

The Controlling component uses orders to plan, monitor and settle operating costs. QM orders are the means by which the activities that are performed during a quality inspection are linked to account assignment objects in the Controlling component. Like all costs accounted for by the Controlling component, an order category classifies the appraisal costs according to the functional origin of the costs. The functional origin of QM quality costs is indicated by the order category 06. In turn, standard QM order for appraisal costs order types or custom order types are used to collect the costs that originate with inspection activities. The type of QM order used can be determined by the assignment of an order type to the material master record inspection type in Customizing. For example, the general QM order for appraisal costs is a long-term cost collector that's created with a manual process and used to collect costs for more than one inspection lot or material. These costs settled periodically. In turn, the individual QM order for appraisal costs is a short-term cost collector that's created automatically and used to collect inspection costs for a single inspection lot or material. These costs are settled on a one-time basis. To account for appraisal costs using an individual QM order for appraisal costs, the order is created as the inspection lot is created. The order is then assigned to the inspection lot. Following the inspection, inspection activities are recorded in the QM order in terms of activity types that are defined for a work center and related activity times as characteristic inspection results are recorded and valuated or as the usage decision for the inspection lot is documented. Next, the CO component retrieves predefined prices for the documented activity types and uses the prices to convert the activity times to actual costs. These appraisal costs are settled to a cost object, such as a cost center or a CO internal order, according to a settlement rule that's defined for the QM order master record. In turn, settlement profiles, which are defined in Customizing, determine the allowed receiver for each order type. When the appraisal costs are settled to cost objects, the system generates offsetting entries to the sender objects, whereas the debit postings remain in place. The confirmation of activities for quality inspection operations requires the creation of activity types for work centers and activity prices in Controlling and the assignment of work centers to cost objects in PP. Activity confirmation also requires the assignment of a work center to a plan operation, the definition of standard values for activity types and the assignment of the QM order to the inspection lot in QM. Also needed is the assignment of a QM order to the inspection lot and the use of an inspection plan for the inspection.

Q-14:   C. One-time cost settlement

The Controlling component uses orders to plan, monitor and settle operating costs. QM orders are the means by which the activities that are performed during a quality inspection are linked to account assignment objects in the Controlling component. Like all costs accounted for by the Controlling component, an order category classifies the appraisal costs according to the functional origin of the costs. The functional origin of QM quality costs is indicated by the order category 06. In turn, standard QM order for appraisal costs order types or custom order types are used to collect the costs that originate with inspection activities. The type of QM order used can be determined by the assignment of an order type to the material master record inspection type in Customizing.   For example, the general QM order for appraisal costs is a long-term cost collector that's created with a manual process and used to collect costs for more than one inspection lot or material. These costs settled periodically. In turn, the individual QM order for appraisal costs is a short-term cost collector that's created automatically and used to collect inspection costs for a single inspection lot or material. These costs are settled on a one-time basis. To account for appraisal costs using an individual QM order for appraisal costs, the order is created as the inspection lot is created. The order is then assigned to the inspection lot. Following the inspection, inspection activities are recorded in the QM order in terms of activity types that are defined for a work center and related activity times as characteristic inspection results are recorded and valuated or as the usage decision for the inspection lot is documented. Next, the CO component retrieves predefined prices for the documented activity types and uses the prices to convert the activity times to actual costs. These appraisal costs are settled to a cost object, such as a cost center or a CO internal order, according to a settlement rule that's defined for the QM order master record. In turn, settlement profiles, which are defined in Customizing, determine the allowed receiver for each order type. For example, the standard settlement receiver control indicator is set in the order if a single settlement of costs to a cost center or CO internal order is desired. When the appraisal costs are settled to cost objects, the system automatically generates offsetting entries to the sender objects whereas the debit postings remain in place.

Q-15:   A. Specify order type for inspection type

The Controlling component uses orders to plan, monitor and settle operating costs. QM orders are the means by which the activities that are performed during a quality inspection are linked to account assignment objects in the Controlling component. Like all costs accounted for by the Controlling component, an order category classifies the appraisal costs according to the functional origin of the costs. The functional origin of QM quality costs is indicated by the order category 06. In turn, standard QM order for appraisal costs order types or custom order types are used to collect the costs that originate with inspection activities. The type of QM order used can be determined by the assignment of an order type to the material master record inspection type in Customizing. For example, the general QM

order for appraisal costs is a long-term cost collector
that's created with a manual process and used to collect
costs for more than one inspection lot or material.
These costs settled periodically. In turn, the individual
QM order for appraisal costs is a short-term cost
collector that's created automatically and used to collect
inspection costs for a single inspection lot or material.
These costs are settled on a one-time basis. To account
for appraisal costs using an individual QM order for
appraisal costs, the order is created as the inspection lot
is created. The order is then assigned to the inspection
lot. Following the inspection, inspection activities are
recorded in the QM order in terms of activity types that
are defined for a work center and related activity times
as characteristic inspection results are recorded and
valuated or as the usage decision for the inspection lot
is documented. Next, the CO component retrieves
predefined prices for the documented activity types and
uses the prices to convert the activity times to actual
costs. These appraisal costs are settled to a cost object,
such as a cost center or a CO internal order, according
to a settlement rule that's defined for the QM order
master record. In turn, settlement profiles, which are
defined in Customizing, determine the allowed receiver
for each order type. When the appraisal costs are settled
to cost objects, the system generates offsetting entries
to the sender objects, whereas the debit postings remain
in place.   The confirmation of activities for quality
inspection operations requires the creation of activity
types for work centers and activity prices in
Controlling and the assignment of work centers to cost
objects in PP. Activity confirmation also requires the
assignment of a work center to a plan operation, the

definition of standard values for activity types and the assignment of the QM order to the inspection lot in QM. Also needed is the assignment of a QM order to the inspection lot and the use of an inspection plan for the inspection.

Q-16:   B. Milestone confirmation indicator for operation control key

The Controlling component uses orders to plan, monitor and settle operating costs. QM orders are the means by which the activities that support the processing of quality inspections are linked to account assignment objects in the Controlling component. The "milestone confirmation" and "confirmation required" control indicators for the operation control key determine if the confirmation of activities for a QM order is required. If so, the system automatically displays a dialog box in which the user can record activities.

Q-17:   C. Order type is assigned to the inspection type in the material master record

The Controlling component uses orders to plan, monitor and settle operating costs. QM orders are the means by which the activities that are performed during a quality inspection are linked to account assignment objects in the Controlling component. Like all costs accounted for by the Controlling component, an order category classifies the appraisal costs according to the functional origin of the costs. The functional origin of QM quality costs is indicated by the order category 06.

143

In turn, standard QM order for appraisal costs order types or custom order types are used to collect the costs that originate with inspection activities. The type of QM order used can be determined by the assignment of an order type to the material master record inspection type in Customizing. For example, the general QM order for appraisal costs is a long-term cost collector that's created with a manual process and used to collect costs for more than one inspection lot or material. These costs settled periodically. In turn, the individual QM order for appraisal costs is a short-term cost collector that's created automatically and used to collect inspection costs for a single inspection lot or material. These costs are settled on a one-time basis. To account for appraisal costs using an individual QM order for appraisal costs, the order is created as the inspection lot is created. The order is then assigned to the inspection lot. Following the inspection, inspection activities are recorded in the QM order in terms of activity types that are defined for a work center and related activity times as characteristic inspection results are recorded and valuated or as the usage decision for the inspection lot is documented. Next, the CO component retrieves predefined prices for the documented activity types and uses the prices to convert the activity times to actual costs. These appraisal costs are settled to a cost object, such as a cost center or a CO internal order, according to a settlement rule that's defined for the QM order master record. In turn, settlement profiles, which are defined in Customizing, determine the allowed receiver for each order type. When the appraisal costs are settled to cost objects, the system generates offsetting entries to the sender objects, whereas the debit postings remain in place. The confirmation of activities for quality inspection operations requires the creation of activity types for work centers and activity prices in Controlling and the assignment of work centers to cost objects in PP. Activity confirmation also requires the assignment of a work center to a plan operation, the definition of standard values for activity types and the assignment of the QM order to the inspection lot in QM. Also needed is the assignment of a QM order to the inspection lot and the use of an inspection plan for the inspection. When an individual QM order for appraisal costs is used, the assignment of the order type to the inspection type in the material master record determines the order type used to document appraisal costs.

Q-18:   C. Nonconformity costs

Efforts made to assure the quality of a product or service result in quality costs. The functions of the Quality Management component lead to the incurrence of two types of quality costs: appraisal costs and nonconformity costs. Nonconformity costs result from the creation of a product or service, the characteristics of which do not conform to defined specifications or standards. Nonconformity costs include the costs of analyzing product and material defects and the completion of activities, which rectify issues that affect product quality. Such costs include defect costs, rework costs and warranty costs.

Q-19:   B. Results Recording and C. Usage Decision

The Controlling component uses orders to plan, monitor and settle operating costs. QM orders are the means by which the activities that are performed during a quality inspection are linked to account assignment objects in the Controlling component. Like all costs accounted for by the Controlling component, an order category classifies the appraisal costs according to the functional origin of the costs. The functional origin of QM quality costs is indicated by the order category 06. In turn, standard QM order for appraisal costs order types or custom order types are used to collect the costs that originate with inspection activities. The type of QM order used can be determined by the assignment of an order type to the material master record inspection type in Customizing. For example, the general QM order for appraisal costs is a long-term cost collector that's created with a manual process and used to collect costs for more than one inspection lot or material. These costs settled periodically. In turn, the individual QM order for appraisal costs is a short-term cost collector that's created automatically and used to collect inspection costs for a single inspection lot or material. These costs are settled on a one-time basis. To account for appraisal costs using an individual QM order for appraisal costs, the order is created as the inspection lot is created. The order is then assigned to the inspection lot. Following the inspection, inspection activities are recorded in the QM order in terms of activity types that are defined for a work center and related activity times as characteristic inspection results are recorded and valuated or as the usage decision for the inspection lot is documented. Next, the CO component retrieves predefined prices for the documented activity types and uses the prices to convert the activity times to actual costs. These appraisal costs are settled to a cost object, such as a cost center or a CO internal order, according to a settlement rule that's defined for the QM order master record. In turn, settlement profiles, which are defined in Customizing, determine the allowed receiver for each order type. When the appraisal costs are settled to cost objects, the system generates offsetting entries to the sender objects, whereas the debit postings remain in place. The Results Recording and Usage Decision functions are used to record activity times that are accounted for by a general QM order for appraisal costs.

Q-20: A. Accumulate appraisal costs for multiple materials using one order

The Controlling component uses orders to plan, monitor and settle operating costs. QM orders are the means by which the activities that are performed during a quality inspection are linked to account assignment objects in the Controlling component. Like all costs accounted for by the Controlling component, an order category classifies the appraisal costs according to the functional origin of the costs. The functional origin of QM quality costs is indicated by the order category 06. In turn, standard QM order for appraisal costs order types or custom order types are used to collect the costs that originate with inspection activities. The type of QM order used can be determined by the assignment of an order type to the material master record inspection type in Customizing. For example, the general QM order for appraisal costs is a long-term cost collector that's created with a manual process and used to collect costs for more than one inspection lot or material. These costs settled periodically. In turn, the individual QM order for appraisal costs is a short-term cost collector that's created automatically and used to collect inspection costs for a single inspection lot or material. These costs are settled on a one-time basis.

Q-21:   B. Multiple inspection lots will be assigned to the QM order

The Controlling component uses orders to plan, monitor and settle operating costs. QM orders are the means by which the activities that are performed during a quality inspection are linked to account assignment objects in the Controlling component. Like all costs accounted for by the Controlling component, an order category classifies the appraisal costs according to the functional origin of the costs. The functional origin of QM quality costs is indicated by the order category 06. In turn, standard QM order for appraisal costs order types or custom order types are used to collect the costs that originate with inspection activities. The type of QM order used can be determined by the assignment of an order type to the material master record inspection type in Customizing. For example, the general QM order for appraisal costs is a long-term cost collector that's created with a manual process and used to collect costs for more than one inspection lot or material. These costs settled periodically. In turn, the individual QM order for appraisal costs is a short-term cost collector that's created automatically and used to collect inspection costs for a single inspection lot or material. These costs are settled on a one-time basis.

Q-22:   B. Display cost report for QM order

The Controlling component uses orders to plan, monitor and settle operating costs. QM orders are the means by which the activities that are performed during a quality inspection are linked to account assignment objects in the Controlling component. The documented appraisal costs data can be evaluated using three different Quality Costs functions: Display QM Orders by Inspection Type, Display Cost Report for QM Order and Display Cost Report for Inspection Lot Confirmed Activities. In particular, the Display Cost Report for QM Order refers to summarized costs for all materials or inspection lots assigned to an individual or a general QM order. The report organizes activity types and the related costs according to individual cost elements. The user can display the data in the list in graphic form or export the cost data to an Excel spreadsheet. The report can also be printed.

Q-23:   A. Plant and D. Order type

The Controlling component uses orders to plan, monitor and settle operating costs. QM orders are the means by which the activities that support the processing of quality inspections are linked to account assignment objects in the Controlling component. If the central maintenance function is used to create and assign a QM order, required entries in the order include plant, inspection type, and/or material and cost object.

Q-24:   A. Material number and C. Inspection type

The Controlling component uses orders to plan, monitor and settle operating costs. QM orders are the means by which the activities that are performed during quality inspections are linked to account assignment objects in the Controlling component. Once the orders are created, the documented appraisal costs data can be evaluated using three different Quality Costs functions: Display QM Orders by Inspection Type, Display Cost Report for QM Order and Display Cost Report for Inspection Lot Confirmed Activities. In particular, the QM Orders by Inspection Type List refers to all materials for which a QM order has been created that meet selection criteria, such as inspection type, material, plant and QM order. The list, which organizes the orders according to material number, includes material short text, inspection type and inspection type description fields. After the list is created, the user can select an order from the list and display the related material master record or the Controlling data.

Q-25:   A. Activity times and C. Activity prices

The Controlling component uses orders to plan, monitor and settle operating costs. QM orders are the means by which the activities that are performed during a quality inspection are linked to account assignment objects in the Controlling component. Like all costs accounted for by the Controlling component, an order category classifies the appraisal costs according to the functional origin of the costs. The functional origin of QM quality costs is indicated by the order category 06.

In turn, standard QM order for appraisal costs order types or custom order types are used to collect the costs that originate with inspection activities. The type of QM order used can be determined by the assignment of an order type to the material master record inspection type in Customizing. For example, the general QM order for appraisal costs is a long-term cost collector that's created with a manual process and used to collect costs for more than one inspection lot or material. These costs settled periodically. In turn, the individual QM order for appraisal costs is a short-term cost collector that's created automatically and used to collect inspection costs for a single inspection lot or material. These costs are settled on a one-time basis. To account for appraisal costs using an individual QM order for appraisal costs, the order is created as the inspection lot is created. The order is then assigned to the inspection lot. Following the inspection, inspection activities are recorded in the QM order in terms of activity types that are defined for a work center and related activity times as characteristic inspection results are recorded and valuated or as the usage decision for the inspection lot is documented. Next, the CO component retrieves predefined prices for the documented activity types and uses the prices to convert the activity times to actual costs. These appraisal costs are settled to a cost object, such as a cost center or a CO internal order, according to a settlement rule that's defined for the QM order master record. In turn, settlement profiles, which are defined in Customizing, determine the allowed receiver for each order type. When the appraisal costs are settled to cost objects, the system generates offsetting entries to the sender objects, whereas the debit postings remain in place.

Q-26:   A. Work center and C. Plant

The Controlling component uses orders to plan, monitor and settle operating costs. QM orders are the means by which the activities that are performed during a quality inspection are linked to account assignment objects in the Controlling component. Like all costs accounted for by the Controlling component, an order category classifies the appraisal costs according to the functional origin of the costs. The functional origin of QM quality costs is indicated by the order category 06. In turn, standard QM order for appraisal costs order types or custom order types are used to collect the costs that originate with inspection activities. The type of QM order used can be determined by the assignment of an order type to the material master record inspection type in Customizing. For example, the general QM order for appraisal costs is a long-term cost collector that's created with a manual process and used to collect costs for more than one inspection lot or material. These costs settled periodically. In turn, the individual QM order for appraisal costs is a short-term cost collector that's created automatically and used to collect inspection costs for a single inspection lot or material. These costs are settled on a one-time basis. To account for appraisal costs using an individual QM order for appraisal costs, the order is created as the inspection lot is created. The order is then assigned to the inspection lot. Following the inspection, inspection activities are recorded in the QM order in terms of activity types that are defined for a work center and related activity times as characteristic inspection results are recorded and valuated or as the usage decision for the inspection lot is documented. Next, the CO component retrieves predefined prices for the documented activity types and uses the prices to convert the activity times to actual costs. These appraisal costs are settled to a cost object, such as a cost center or a CO internal order, according to a settlement rule that's defined for the QM order master record. In turn, settlement profiles, which are defined in Customizing, determine the allowed receiver for each order type. When the appraisal costs are settled to cost objects, the system generates offsetting entries to the sender objects, whereas the debit postings remain in place. To confirm appraisal activities during the results recording process requires the definition of activity types for each work center and prices for activity types in Controlling. Also required are the assignment of work centers to cost objects in PP, the assignment of work centers to inspection plan operations, the definition of standard values for activity types and the assignment of a QM order to the inspection lot.

Q-27:   C. Nonconformity costs

Efforts made to assure the quality of a product or service result in quality costs. The functions of the Quality Management component lead to the incurrence of two types of quality costs: appraisal costs and nonconformity costs. Nonconformity costs result from the creation of a product or service, the characteristics of which do not conform to defined specifications or standards. Nonconformity costs include the costs of analyzing product and material defects and the completion of activities, which rectify issues that affect product quality. Such costs include defect costs, rework costs and warranty costs.

Q-28:   B. Rework costs and D. Warranty costs

Efforts made to assure the quality of a product or service result in quality costs. The functions of the Quality Management component lead to the incurrence of two types of quality costs: appraisal costs and nonconformity costs. Nonconformity costs result from the creation of a product or service, the characteristics of which do not conform to defined specifications or standards. Nonconformity costs include the costs of analyzing product and material defects and the completion of activities, which rectify issues that affect product quality. Such costs include defect costs, rework costs and warranty costs.

Q-29:   A. Order category

The Controlling component uses orders to plan, monitor and settle operating costs. QM orders are the means by which the activities that support the processing of quality inspections and notifications are linked to cost assignment objects in the Controlling component. Like all costs accounted for by the Controlling component, nonconformity costs are classified according to the functional origin of the costs. This functional origin is represented by the order category, which is assigned to the order by the

Controlling component. For example, the order category 06 is used to categorize quality-cost related orders that originate with the QM application. The order category is maintained in the Controlling component.

Q-30:   D. Activity types and E. Activity times

The Controlling component uses orders to plan, monitor and settle operating costs. QM orders are the means by which the activities that are performed during a quality inspection are linked to account assignment objects in the Controlling component. Like all costs accounted for by the Controlling component, an order category classifies the appraisal costs according to the functional origin of the costs. The functional origin of QM quality costs is indicated by the order category 06. In turn, standard QM order for appraisal costs order types or custom order types are used to collect the costs that originate with inspection activities. The type of QM order used can be determined by the assignment of an order type to the material master record inspection type in Customizing. For example, the individual QM order for appraisal costs is a short-term cost collector that's created automatically and used to collect inspection costs for a single inspection lot or material. These costs are settled on a one-time basis. To account for appraisal costs using an individual QM order for appraisal costs, the order is created as the inspection lot is created. The order is then assigned to the inspection lot. Following the inspection, inspection activities are recorded in the QM order in terms of activity types that are defined for a work center and related activity times as characteristic inspection results are recorded and valuated, or as the usage decision for the inspection lot is documented. Next, the CO component retrieves predefined prices for the documented activity types and uses the prices to convert the activity times to actual costs. These appraisal costs are settled to a cost object, such as a cost center or a CO internal order, according to a settlement rule that's defined for the QM order master record. When the appraisal costs are settled to cost objects, the system generates offsetting entries to the sender objects, whereas the debit postings remain in place.

Q-31:   A. Create QM Order, C. Replace QM Order and D. Confirm Activities

Efforts made to assure the quality of a product or service result in quality costs. The functions of the Quality Management component lead to the incurrence of two types of quality costs: appraisal costs and nonconformity costs. Nonconformity costs result from the creation of a product or service, the characteristics of which do not conform to defined specifications or standards. Such costs include defect costs, rework costs and warranty costs. In turn, appraisal costs result from the performance of inspections that confirm the quality of products and the conformance of the products to established benchmarks. Such costs include labor, material and equipment costs. Functions that support the documentation and management of both appraisal and nonconformity costs include the Create, Copy, Replace or Delete QM Order functions, the Assign QM Order function, the Confirm Activities function and the QM Order Evaluations functions.

Q-32:   B. Order type

The Controlling component uses orders to plan, monitor and settle operating costs. QM orders are the means by which the activities that support the processing of quality inspections and notifications are linked to cost assignment objects in the Controlling component. Like all costs accounted for by the Controlling component, Like all costs accounted for by the CO component, appraisal and nonconformity costs are classified according to the functional origin of the costs by means of an order category. The functional origin of quality costs is indicated by the order category 06. In turn, the QM order for inspection costs order types are used to collect costs that originate with the inspection activities and the QM order type for nonconformity costs is used to collect costs that originate with notification-processing activities.

Q-33:   A. Link QM order to account assignment object

The Controlling component uses orders to plan, monitor and settle operating costs. QM orders are the means by which the activities that support the processing of quality inspections are linked to account assignment objects in the Controlling component. Like all costs accounted for by the Controlling component, an order category classifies the appraisal costs according to the functional origin of the costs. The functional origin of QM quality costs is indicated by the order category 06. In turn, standard QM order for appraisal costs order types or custom order types are used to collect the costs that originate with inspection activities. Inspection activities are recorded in the QM appraisal order in terms of activity types and activity times. The CO component retrieves predefined prices for the documented activity types and uses the prices to convert the activity times to actual costs. These inspection costs are then settled to one or more cost objects, such as a cost center or a CO internal order according to the settlement rule that's defined for the QM order. In turn, the system automatically generates offsetting entries to the sender objects, whereas the debit postings remain in place. The system then automatically generates offsetting entries to the sender objects and the debit postings to the sender object remain in place.

Q-34:   C. Nonconformity costs

Efforts made to assure the quality of a product or service result in quality costs. The functions of the Quality Management component lead to the incurrence of two types of quality costs: appraisal costs and nonconformity costs. Nonconformity costs result from the creation of a product or service, the characteristics of which do not conform to defined specifications or standards. Nonconformity costs include the costs of analyzing product and material defects and the completion of activities, which rectify issues that affect product quality. Such costs include defect costs, rework costs and warranty costs.

Q-35:   C. Costs incurred to correct nonconformities of products

Efforts made to assure the quality of a product or service result in quality costs. The functions of the Quality Management component lead to the incurrence of two types of quality costs: appraisal costs and nonconformity costs. Nonconformity costs result from the creation of a product or service, the characteristics of which do not conform to defined specifications or standards. Nonconformity costs include the costs of analyzing product and material defects and the completion of activities, which rectify issues that affect product quality. Such costs include defect costs, rework costs and warranty costs.

Q-36:   B. Material used in an inspection and D. Test equipment

Efforts made to assure the quality of a product or service result in quality costs. The functions of the Quality Management component lead to the incurrence of two types of quality costs: appraisal costs and nonconformity costs. Nonconformity costs result from the creation of a product or service, the characteristics of which do not conform to defined specifications or standards. Such costs include defect costs, rework costs and warranty costs. In turn, appraisal costs result from the performance of inspections that confirm the quality of products and the conformance of the products to established benchmarks. Such costs include labor, material and equipment costs.

Q-37:   B. Nonconformity costs

Efforts made to assure the quality of a product or service result in quality costs. The functions of the Quality Management component lead to the incurrence of two types of quality costs: appraisal costs and nonconformity costs. Nonconformity costs result from the creation of a product or service, the characteristics of which do not conform to defined specifications or standards. Nonconformity costs include the costs of analyzing product and material defects and the completion of activities, which rectify issues that affect product quality. Such costs include defect costs, rework costs and warranty costs.

Q-38:   B. Short-term cost collector and C. Collects costs for one material or one inspection lot to which it is assigned

The Controlling component uses orders to plan, monitor and settle operating costs. QM orders are the means by which the activities that are performed during a quality inspection are linked to account assignment objects in the Controlling component. Like all costs accounted for by the Controlling component, an order category classifies the appraisal costs according to the functional origin of the costs. The functional origin of QM quality costs is indicated by the order category 06. In turn, standard QM order for appraisal costs order types or custom order types are used to collect the costs that originate with inspection activities. The type of QM order used can be determined by the assignment of an order type to the material master record inspection type in Customizing. For example, the individual QM order for appraisal costs is a short-term cost collector that's created automatically and used to collect inspection costs for a single inspection lot or material. These costs are settled on a one-time basis. To account for appraisal costs using an individual QM order for appraisal costs, the order is created as the inspection lot is created. The order is then assigned to the inspection lot. Following the inspection, inspection activities are recorded in the QM order in terms of activity types that are defined for a work center and related activity times as characteristic inspection results are recorded and valuated, or as the usage decision for the inspection lot is documented. Next, the CO component retrieves predefined prices for the documented activity types and uses the prices to convert the activity times to actual costs. These appraisal costs are settled to a cost object, such as a cost center or a CO internal order, according to a settlement rule that's defined for the QM order master record. When the appraisal costs are settled to cost objects, the system generates offsetting entries to the sender objects, whereas the debit postings remain in place.

Q-39:   C. Determine parameters that control how the order is processed

The Controlling component uses orders to plan, monitor and settle operating costs. QM orders are the means by which the activities that are performed during a quality inspection are linked to account assignment objects in the Controlling component. Like all costs accounted for by the Controlling component, an order category classifies the appraisal costs according to the functional origin of the costs. The functional origin of QM quality costs is indicated by the order category 06. In turn, standard QM order for appraisal costs order types or custom order types are used to collect the costs that originate with inspection activities. The type of QM order used can be determined by the assignment of an order type to the material master record inspection type in Customizing. For example, the general QM order for appraisal costs is a long-term cost collector that's created with a manual process and used to collect costs for more than one inspection lot or material. These costs settled periodically. In turn, the individual QM order for appraisal costs is a short-term cost collector that's created automatically and used to collect inspection costs for a single inspection lot or material. These costs are settled on a one-time basis. To account for appraisal costs using an individual QM order for appraisal costs, the order is created as the inspection lot is created. The order is then assigned to the inspection lot. Following the inspection, inspection activities are recorded in the QM order in terms of activity types that are defined for a work center and related activity times as characteristic inspection results are recorded and valuated or as the usage decision for the inspection lot is documented. Next, the CO component retrieves predefined prices for the documented activity types and uses the prices to convert the activity times to actual costs. These appraisal costs are settled to a cost object, such as a cost center or a CO internal order, according to a settlement rule that's defined for the QM order master record. In turn, settlement profiles, which are defined in Customizing, determine the allowed receiver for each order type. When the appraisal costs are settled to cost objects, the system generates offsetting entries to the sender objects, whereas the debit postings remain in place.

Q-40:   B. QM order type QL02

The Controlling component uses orders to plan, monitor and settle operating costs. QM orders are the means by which the activities that are performed during a quality inspection are linked to account assignment objects in the Controlling component. Like all costs accounted for by the Controlling component, an order category classifies the appraisal costs according to the functional origin of the costs. The functional origin of QM quality costs is indicated by the order category 06. In turn, standard QM order for appraisal costs order types or custom order types are used to collect the costs that originate with inspection activities. The type of QM order used can be determined by the assignment of an order type to the material master record inspection type in Customizing. For example, the general QM order for appraisal costs, QL01, is a long-term cost collector that's created with a manual process and used to collect costs for more than one inspection lot or material. These costs settled periodically. In turn, the individual QM order for appraisal costs, QL02, is a short-term cost collector that's created automatically and used to collect inspection costs for a single inspection lot or material. These costs are settled on a one-time basis.

Q-41:   A. Assign order type to the notification type and D. Assign account assignment object to the order type

The Controlling component uses orders to plan, monitor and settle operating costs. The QM order that's assigned to a notification is the means by which activities that support the processing of quality notifications are linked to cost assignment objects in the Controlling component. Like all costs accounted for by the Controlling component, nonconformity costs are classified according to the functional origin of the costs by means of an order category. The functional origin of quality costs is indicated by the order category 06. In turn, a new or existing QM order for nonconformity costs order type, QN03, is created manually and used to collect costs that originate with the activities that are performed as the notification is processed. Each activity is recorded in terms of an activity type and activity times. The CO component then retrieves the predefined prices associated with the activity types for which the activity times were recorded in QM. The CO component converts the activity times to an actual cost on the basis of the predefined prices stored in the CO component. The expenses that are incurred to process the notification are then settled to a cost object, such as a cost center or controlling area, according to the account assignment that is entered when the QM order was created. The system then automatically generates offsetting entries to the sender objects and the debit postings to the sender object remain in place. Requirements for this functionality include the assignment of an order type to a notification type and the assignment of an account assignment object to an order type

Q-42:   C. Change Notification function

The Controlling component uses orders assigned to the notification to plan, monitor and settle nonconformity costs. The QM order for notifications is the means by which notification processing activities are linked to cost assignment objects in the Controlling component. Like all costs accounted for by the Controlling component, notification costs are classified according to the functional origin of the costs by means of an order category. The functional origin of quality costs is represented by the order category 06. In turn, a new or existing QM order for nonconformity costs order type, QN03, is used to collect notification processing costs. Each activity performed to process the notification is recorded in terms of an activity type and activity times. Next, the CO component identifies the predefined price associated with the activity type for which the activity times were recorded in QM. The CO component converts the activity times to an actual cost on the basis of the predefined prices stored in the CO component. The nonconformity costs incurred to process the notification are settled to one or more cost objects, such as cost center or controlling area, according to the account assignment that is entered when the QM order was created. The system automatically generates offsetting entries to the sender objects and the debit postings to the sender object remain in place. The Change Quality Notification function is used to create a QM order for nonconformity costs and assign it to the notification.

Q-43:   B. Settlement of costs to multiple receivers or an account assignment object according to a distribution rule

The Controlling component uses orders to plan, monitor and settle operating costs. The QM order is the means by which activities that are performed during a quality inspection are linked to cost accounting objects in the Controlling component. These activities are recorded in the QM order in terms of activity types and activity times using the QM component. The Controlling component then retrieves the predefined prices for the documented activity types and uses the prices to convert recorded activity times to actual costs. The costs are then settled to one or more cost objects according to the account assignments entered when the QM order was created. For example, the standard settlement receiver control indicator is set in the order if a single settlement of costs to a cost center or CO internal order is desired. The special settlement rule control indicator is set if a distribution rule is used to settle costs to several receivers.

Q-44:   A. Special settlement rule control indicator is selected during the creation of the order

The Controlling component uses orders to plan, monitor and settle operating costs. The QM order is the means by which activities that are performed during a quality inspection are linked to cost accounting

166

objects in the Controlling component. These activities are recorded in the QM order in terms of activity types and activity times using the QM component. The Controlling component then retrieves the predefined prices for the documented activity types and uses the prices to convert recorded activity times to actual costs. The costs are then settled to one or more cost objects according to the account assignments entered when the QM order was created. For example, the standard settlement receiver control indicator is set in the order if a single settlement of costs to a cost center or CO internal order is desired. The special settlement rule control indicator is set if a distribution rule is used to settle costs to several receivers.

Q-45:   A. True

A benefit of the use of an individual QM order for appraisal costs versus a general QM order for appraisal costs is the ability to trace appraisal costs to an individual material or inspection lot

Q-46:   A. Results Recording and C. Usage Decision

The Controlling component uses orders to plan, monitor and settle operating costs. QM orders are the means by which the activities that are performed during a quality inspection are linked to account assignment objects in the Controlling component. Like all costs accounted for by the Controlling component, an order category classifies the appraisal costs according to the functional origin of the costs. The functional origin of QM quality costs is indicated by the order category 06.

In turn, standard QM order for appraisal costs order types or custom order types are used to collect the costs that originate with inspection activities. For example, the individual QM order for appraisal costs is a short-term cost collector that's created automatically and used to collect inspection costs for a single inspection lot or material. These costs are settled on a one-time basis. To account for appraisal costs using an individual QM order for appraisal costs, the order is created as the inspection lot is created. The order is then assigned to the inspection lot. Following the inspection, inspection activities are recorded in the QM order in terms of activity types that are defined for a work center and related activity times as characteristic inspection results are recorded and valuated or as the usage decision for the inspection lot is documented. Next, the CO component retrieves predefined prices for the documented activity types and uses the prices to convert the activity times to actual costs. These appraisal costs are settled to a cost object, such as a cost center or a CO internal order, according to a settlement rule that's defined for the QM order master record. In turn, settlement profiles, which are defined in Customizing, determine the allowed receiver for each order type. When the appraisal costs are settled to cost objects, the system generates offsetting entries to the sender objects, whereas the debit postings remain in place. Both the Results Recording and the Usage Decision functions can be used to confirm activities for inspection operations.

Q-47:   B. Assign appraisal costs to individual material and C. Collect appraisal costs on short-term basis

The Controlling component uses orders to plan, monitor and settle operating costs. QM orders are the means by which the activities that are performed during a quality inspection are linked to account assignment objects in the Controlling component. Like all costs accounted for by the Controlling component, an order category classifies the appraisal costs according to the functional origin of the costs. The functional origin of QM quality costs is indicated by the order category 06. In turn, standard QM order for appraisal costs order types or custom order types are used to collect the costs that originate with inspection activities. For example, the individual QM order for appraisal costs is a short-term cost collector that's created automatically and used to collect inspection costs for a single inspection lot or material. These costs are settled on a one-time basis. To account for appraisal costs using an individual QM order for appraisal costs, the order is created as the inspection lot is created. The order is then assigned to the inspection lot. Following the inspection, inspection activities are recorded in the QM order in terms of activity types that are defined for a work center and related activity times as characteristic inspection results are recorded and valuated or as the usage decision for the inspection lot is documented. Next, the CO component retrieves predefined prices for the documented activity types and uses the prices to convert the activity times to actual costs. These appraisal costs are settled to a cost object, such as a cost center or a CO internal order, according to a settlement rule that's defined for the QM order master record. In turn, settlement profiles, which are defined in

Customizing, determine the allowed receiver for each order type. When the appraisal costs are settled to cost objects, the system generates offsetting entries to the sender objects, whereas the debit postings remain in place.

Q-48:   A. Inspection operation in QM Customizing application

The Controlling component uses orders to plan, monitor and settle operating costs. QM orders are the means by which the activities that support the processing of quality inspections are linked to account assignment objects in the Controlling component. The milestone confirmation and confirmation required control indicators for the operation control key determine if the confirmation of activities for a QM order is required. If so, the system automatically displays a dialog box in which the user can record inspection activities and activity times.

Q-49:   A. Milestone confirmation control indicator for operation control key

The Controlling component uses orders to plan, monitor and settle operating costs. QM orders are the means by which the activities that support the processing of quality inspections are linked to account assignment objects in the Controlling component. The milestone confirmation and confirmation required control indicators for the operation control key determine if the confirmation of activities for a QM order is required. If so, the system automatically displays a dialog box in which the user can record inspection activities and activity times.

Q-50:   A. Order is cost collector for one or more materials or inspection lots and B. Order is short-term or long-term cost collector

The Controlling component uses orders to plan, monitor and settle operating costs. QM orders are the means by which the activities that are performed during a quality inspection are linked to account assignment objects in the Controlling component. Like all costs accounted for by the Controlling component, an order category classifies the appraisal costs according to the functional origin of the costs. The functional origin of QM quality costs is indicated by the order category 06. In turn, standard QM order for appraisal costs order types or custom order types are used to collect the costs that originate with inspection activities. For example, the individual QM order for appraisal costs is a short-term cost collector that's created automatically and used to collect inspection costs for a single inspection lot or material. These costs are settled on a one-time basis. To account for appraisal costs using an individual QM order for appraisal costs, the order is created as the inspection lot is created. The order is then assigned to the inspection lot. Following the inspection, inspection activities are recorded in the QM order in terms of activity types that are defined for a work center and related activity times as characteristic inspection results are recorded and valuated or as the usage decision for the inspection lot is documented. Next, the CO component retrieves predefined prices for the documented activity types and uses the prices to convert the activity times to actual costs. These appraisal costs are settled to a cost object, such as a cost center or a CO internal order, according to a settlement rule that's defined for the QM order master record. In turn, settlement profiles, which are defined in Customizing, determine the allowed receiver for each order type. When the appraisal costs are settled to cost objects, the system generates offsetting entries to the sender objects, whereas the debit postings remain in place.

Q-51:   A. Labor costs and C. Material costs

Efforts made to assure the quality of a product or service result in quality costs. The functions of the Quality Management component lead to the incurrence of two types of quality costs: appraisal costs and nonconformity costs. Nonconformity costs result from the creation of a product or service, the characteristics of which do not conform to defined specifications or standards. Such costs include defect costs, rework costs and warranty costs. In turn, appraisal costs result from the performance of inspections that confirm the quality of products and the conformance of the products to established benchmarks. Such costs include labor, material and equipment costs.

Q-52:   B. QM orders by inspection type report

The Controlling component uses orders to plan, monitor and settle operating costs. QM orders are the means by which the activities that are performed during quality inspections are linked to account assignment objects in the Controlling component. Once the orders are created, the documented appraisal costs data can be evaluated using three different Quality Costs functions: Display QM Orders by Inspection Type, Display Cost Report for QM Order and Display Cost Report for Inspection Lot Confirmed Activities. In particular, the QM Orders by Inspection Type List refers to all materials for which a QM order has been created that meet selection criteria, such as inspection type, material, plant and QM order. The list, which organizes the orders according to material number, includes material short text, inspection type and inspection type description fields. After the list is created, the user can select an order from the list and display the related material master record or the Controlling data.

Q-53:   A. Yes

The Controlling component uses orders to plan, monitor and settle operating costs. QM orders are the means by which the activities that are performed during a quality inspection are linked to account assignment objects in the Controlling component. Like all costs accounted for by the Controlling component, an order category classifies the appraisal costs according to the functional origin of the costs. The functional origin of QM quality costs is indicated by the order category 06. In turn, standard QM order for appraisal costs order types or custom order types are used to collect the costs that originate with inspection activities. The type of QM order used can be determined by the assignment of an order type to the material master record inspection type in Customizing. For example, the general QM order for appraisal costs, QL01, is a long-term cost collector that's created with a manual process and used to collect costs for more than one inspection lot or material. These costs settled periodically. In turn, the individual QM order for appraisal costs, QL02, is a short-term cost collector that's created automatically and used to collect inspection costs for a single inspection lot or material. These costs are settled on a one-time basis. Also, custom order types can be defined.

Q-54:   A. General QM order

The Controlling component uses orders to plan, monitor and settle operating costs. QM orders are the means by which the activities that are performed during a quality inspection are linked to account assignment objects in the Controlling component. Like all costs accounted for by the Controlling component, an order category classifies the appraisal costs according to the functional origin of the costs. The functional origin of QM quality costs is indicated by the order category 06. In turn, standard QM order for appraisal costs order types or custom order types are used to collect the costs that originate with inspection activities. The type of QM order used can be determined by the assignment of an order type to the material master record inspection type in Customizing. For example, the general QM order for appraisal costs, QL01, is a long-term cost collector that's created with a manual process and used to collect costs for more than one inspection lot or material. These costs settled periodically. In turn, the individual QM order for appraisal costs, QL02, is a short-term cost collector that's created automatically and used to collect inspection costs for a single inspection lot or material. These costs are settled on a one-time basis. Also, custom order types can be defined.

Q-55:   A. The need does not exist to collect costs for a number of materials and B. The need exists to assign the accumulated costs to particular materials or inspection lots

The Controlling component uses orders to plan, monitor and settle operating costs. QM orders are the means by which the activities that are performed during a quality inspection are linked to account assignment objects in the Controlling component. Like all costs accounted for by the Controlling component, an order category classifies the appraisal costs according to the functional origin of the costs. The functional origin of QM quality costs is indicated by the order category 06. In turn, standard QM order for appraisal costs order types or custom order types are used to collect the costs that originate with inspection activities. The type of QM order used can be determined by the assignment of an order type to the material master record inspection type in Customizing. For example, the general QM order for appraisal costs, QL01, is a long-term cost collector that's created with a manual process and used to collect costs for more than one inspection lot or material. These costs settled periodically. In turn, the individual QM order for appraisal costs, QL02, is a short-term cost collector that's created automatically and used to collect inspection costs for a single inspection lot or material. These costs are settled on a one-time basis. Also, custom order types can be defined.

Q-56: B. List of orders for a specific material, plant and/or inspection type

The Controlling component uses orders to plan, monitor and settle operating costs. QM orders are the means by which the activities that are performed during quality inspections are linked to account assignment objects in the Controlling component. Once the orders are created, the documented appraisal costs data can be evaluated using three different Quality Costs functions: Display QM Orders by Inspection Type, Display Cost Report for QM Order and Display Cost Report for Inspection Lot Confirmed Activities. In particular, the QM Orders by Inspection Type List refers to all materials for which a QM order has been created that meet selection criteria, such as inspection type, material, plant and QM order. The list, which organizes the orders according to material number, includes material short text, inspection type and inspection type description fields. After the list is created, the user can select an order from the list and display the related material master record or the Controlling data.

Q-57: A. True

The Controlling component uses orders to plan, monitor and settle operating costs. QM orders are the

means by which the activities that are performed during a quality inspection are linked to account assignment objects in the Controlling component. Like all costs accounted for by the Controlling component, an order category classifies the appraisal costs according to the functional origin of the costs. The functional origin of QM quality costs is indicated by the order category 06. In turn, standard QM order for appraisal costs order types or custom order types are used to collect the costs that originate with inspection activities. The type of QM order used can be determined by the assignment of an order type to the material master record inspection type in Customizing. For example, the general QM order for appraisal costs, QL01, is a long-term cost collector that's created with a manual process and used to collect costs for more than one inspection lot or material. These costs settled periodically. In turn, the individual QM order for appraisal costs, QL02, is a short-term cost collector that's created automatically and used to collect inspection costs for a single inspection lot or material. These costs are settled on a one-time basis. Also, custom order types can be defined.

Q-58:   A. Activity type and D. Activity price

The Controlling component uses orders to plan, monitor and settle operating costs. QM orders are the means by which the activities that are performed during a quality inspection are linked to account assignment objects in the Controlling component. Like all costs accounted for by the Controlling component, an order category classifies the appraisal costs according to the functional origin of the costs. The functional origin of QM quality costs is indicated by the order category 06. In turn, standard QM order for appraisal costs order types or custom order types are used to collect the costs that originate with inspection activities. For example, the individual QM order for appraisal costs is a short-term cost collector that's created automatically and used to collect inspection costs for a single inspection lot or material. These costs are settled on a one-time basis. To account for appraisal costs using an individual QM order for appraisal costs, the order is created as the inspection lot is created. The order is then assigned to the inspection lot. Following the inspection, inspection activities are recorded in the QM order in terms of activity types that are defined for a work center and related activity times as characteristic inspection results are recorded and valuated or as the usage decision for the inspection lot is documented. Next, the CO component retrieves predefined prices for the documented activity types and uses the prices to convert the activity times to actual costs. These appraisal costs are settled to a cost object, such as a cost center or a CO internal order, according to a settlement rule that's defined for the QM order master record. In turn, settlement profiles, which are defined in Customizing, determine the allowed receiver for each order type. When the appraisal costs are settled to cost objects, the system generates offsetting entries to the sender objects, whereas the debit postings remain in place.

Q-59:   B. Activity type price

The Controlling component uses orders to plan, monitor and settle operating costs. QM orders are the means by which the activities that are performed during a quality inspection are linked to account assignment objects in the Controlling component. Like all costs accounted for by the Controlling component, an order category classifies the appraisal costs according to the functional origin of the costs. The functional origin of QM quality costs is indicated by the order category 06. In turn, standard QM order for appraisal costs order types or custom order types are used to collect the costs that originate with inspection activities. For example, the individual QM order for appraisal costs is a short-term cost collector that's created automatically and used to collect inspection costs for a single inspection lot or material. These costs are settled on a one-time basis. To account for appraisal costs using an individual QM order for appraisal costs, the order is created as the inspection lot is created. The order is then assigned to the inspection lot. Following the inspection, inspection activities are recorded in the QM order in terms of activity types that are defined for a work center and related activity times as characteristic inspection results are recorded and valuated or as the usage decision for the inspection lot is documented. Next, the CO component retrieves predefined prices for the documented activity types and uses the prices to convert the activity times to actual costs. These appraisal costs are settled to a cost object, such as a cost center or a CO internal order, according to a settlement rule that's defined for the QM order master record. In turn, settlement profiles, which are defined in Customizing, determine the allowed receiver for each order type. When the appraisal costs are settled to cost objects, the system generates offsetting entries to the sender objects, whereas the debit postings remain in place.

Q-60:   C. Activity confirmation for inspection operation

The Controlling component uses orders to plan, monitor and settle operating costs. QM orders are the means by which the activities that support the processing of quality inspections are linked to account assignment objects in the Controlling component. Like all costs accounted for by the CO component, appraisal and nonconformity costs are classified according to the functional origin of the costs by means of an order category. The functional origin of quality costs is indicated by the order category 06. In turn, standard QM order for appraisal costs order types or custom order types are used to collect the costs that originate with inspection activities.   To account for quality costs, activities are recorded in QM orders in terms of activity types and activity times. The CO component then retrieves predefined prices for the documented activity types and uses the prices to convert the activity times to actual costs. These inspection costs are subsequently settled to cost objects, such as a cost center or a CO internal order, according to account assignments entered when the QM orders were created. In turn, the system automatically generates offsetting entries to the sender objects, whereas the debit postings remain in place.

Q-61:   B. Determines the account assignment for the QM order

The Controlling component uses orders to plan, monitor and settle operating costs. QM orders are the means by which the activities that support the processing of quality inspections are linked to account assignment objects in the Controlling component. Like all costs accounted for by the CO component, appraisal and nonconformity costs are classified according to the functional origin of the costs by means of an order category. The functional origin of quality costs is indicated by the order category 06. In turn, standard QM order for appraisal costs order types or custom order types are used to collect the costs that originate with inspection activities. To account for quality costs, activities are recorded in QM orders in terms of activity types and activity times. The CO component then retrieves predefined prices for the documented activity types and uses the prices to convert the activity times to actual costs. These inspection costs are subsequently settled to cost objects, such as a cost center or a CO internal order, according to account assignments entered when the QM orders were created. For example, the standard settlement receiver control indicator is set in the order if a single settlement of costs to a cost center or CO internal order is desired. The special settlement rule control indicator is set if a distribution rule is used to settle costs to several receivers. In turn, the system automatically generates offsetting entries to the sender objects, whereas the debit postings remain in place.

Q-62:   B. Special settlement rule control indicator is selected in the QM order

The Controlling component uses orders to plan, monitor and settle operating costs. QM orders are the means by which the activities that support the processing of quality inspections are linked to account assignment objects in the Controlling component. Like all costs accounted for by the CO component, appraisal and nonconformity costs are classified according to the functional origin of the costs by means of an order category. The functional origin of quality costs is indicated by the order category 06. In turn, standard QM order for appraisal costs order types or custom order types are used to collect the costs that originate with inspection activities.   To account for quality costs, activities are recorded in QM orders in terms of activity types and activity times. The CO component then retrieves predefined prices for the documented activity types and uses the prices to convert the activity times to actual costs. These inspection costs are subsequently settled to cost objects, such as a cost center or a CO internal order, according to account assignments entered when the QM orders were created. For example, the standard settlement receiver control indicator is set in the order if a single settlement of costs to a cost center or CO internal order is desired. The special settlement rule control indicator is set if a distribution rule is used to settle costs to several receivers. In turn, the system automatically generates offsetting entries to the sender objects, whereas the debit postings remain in place.

182

Q-63:   B. Assign QM order to inspection lot and C.
Define prices in CO

The Controlling component uses orders to plan,
monitor and settle operating costs. QM orders are the
means by which the activities that support the
processing of quality inspections are linked to account
assignment objects in the Controlling component. Like
all costs accounted for by the CO component, appraisal
and nonconformity costs are classified according to the
functional origin of the costs by means of an order
category. The functional origin of quality costs is
indicated by the order category 06. In turn, standard
QM order for appraisal costs order types or custom
order types are used to collect the costs that originate
with inspection activities.   To account for quality
costs, activities are recorded in QM orders in terms of
activity types and activity times. The CO component
then retrieves predefined prices for the documented
activity types and uses the prices to convert the activity
times to actual costs. These inspection costs are
subsequently settled to cost objects, such as a cost
center or a CO internal order, according to account
assignments entered when the QM orders were created.
For example, the standard settlement receiver control
indicator is set in the order if a single settlement of
costs to a cost center or CO internal order is desired.
The special settlement rule control indicator is set if a
distribution rule is used to settle costs to several
receivers. In turn, the system automatically generates
offsetting entries to the sender objects, whereas the
debit postings remain in place. The confirmation of
activities for quality inspection operations requires the

creation of activity types for work centers and activity prices in Controlling, as well as the assignment of work centers to cost objects in PP. Activity confirmation also requires the assignment of a work center to a plan operation, the definition of standard values for activity types and the assignment of the QM order to the inspection lot in QM. Also needed is the assignment of a QM order to the inspection lot and the use of an inspection plan for the inspection.

Q-64:   B. Results Recording function and C. Usage Decision function

The Controlling component uses orders to plan, monitor and settle operating costs. QM orders are the means by which the activities that support the processing of quality inspections are linked to account assignment objects in the Controlling component. Like all costs accounted for by the CO component, appraisal and nonconformity costs are classified according to the functional origin of the costs by means of an order category. The functional origin of quality costs is indicated by the order category 06. In turn, standard QM order for appraisal costs order types or custom order types are used to collect the costs that originate with inspection activities.   To account for quality costs, activities are recorded in QM orders in terms of activity types and activity times. The CO component then retrieves predefined prices for the documented activity types and uses the prices to convert the activity times to actual costs. These inspection costs are subsequently settled to cost objects, such as a cost center or a CO internal order, according to account assignments entered when the QM orders were created. In turn, the system automatically generates offsetting entries to the sender objects, whereas the debit postings remain in place. Both the Results Recording and the Usage Decision functions can be used to confirm activities for inspection operations.

Q-65:   A. Work center

The Controlling component uses orders to plan, monitor and settle operating costs. QM orders are the means by which the activities that support the processing of quality inspections are linked to account assignment objects in the Controlling component. Like all costs accounted for by the CO component, appraisal and nonconformity costs are classified according to the functional origin of the costs by means of an order category. The functional origin of quality costs is indicated by the order category 06. In turn, standard QM order for appraisal costs order types or custom order types are used to collect the costs that originate with inspection activities. To account for quality costs, activities are recorded in QM orders in terms of activity types and activity times. The CO component then retrieves predefined prices for the documented activity types and uses the prices to convert the activity times to actual costs. These inspection costs are subsequently settled to cost objects, such as a cost center or a CO internal order, according to account assignments entered when the QM orders were created. In turn, the system automatically generates offsetting entries to the sender objects, whereas the debit postings remain in place. The appraisal costs for one inspection operation are differentiated from another on the basis of the work center documented as the order is created.

Q-66:   A. Results Recording and B. Usage Decision

The Controlling component uses orders to plan, monitor and settle operating costs. QM orders are the means by which the activities that support the processing of quality inspections are linked to account assignment objects in the Controlling component. Like all costs accounted for by the CO component, appraisal and nonconformity costs are classified according to the functional origin of the costs by means of an order category. The functional origin of quality costs is indicated by the order category 06. In turn, standard QM order for appraisal costs order types or custom order types are used to collect the costs that originate with inspection activities.   To account for quality costs, activities are recorded in QM orders in terms of activity types and activity times. The CO component then retrieves predefined prices for the documented activity types and uses the prices to convert the activity times to actual costs. These inspection costs are subsequently settled to cost objects, such as a cost center or a CO internal order, according to account assignments entered when the QM orders were created. In turn, the system automatically generates offsetting entries to the sender objects, whereas the debit postings remain in place. Both the Results Recording and the Usage Decision functions can be used to confirm activities for inspection operations, including set-up and labor time incurred during the inspection of a material.

Q-67:   A. Material and C. Labor

Efforts made to assure the quality of a product or service result in quality costs. The functions of the Quality Management component lead to the incurrence of two types of quality costs: appraisal costs and nonconformity costs. Nonconformity costs result from the creation of a product or service, the characteristics of which do not conform to defined specifications or standards. Such costs include defect costs, rework costs and warranty costs. In turn, appraisal costs result from the performance of inspections that confirm the quality of products and the conformance of the products to established benchmarks. Such costs include labor, material and equipment costs.

Q-68:   A. Individual QM order for appraisal costs

The Controlling component uses orders to plan, monitor and settle operating costs. QM orders are the means by which the activities that are performed during a quality inspection are linked to account assignment objects in the Controlling component. Like all costs accounted for by the Controlling component, an order category classifies the appraisal costs according to the functional origin of the costs. The functional origin of QM quality costs is indicated by the order category 06. In turn, standard QM order for appraisal costs order types or custom order types are used to collect the costs that originate with inspection activities. For example, the individual QM order for appraisal costs is a short-term cost collector that's created automatically and used to collect inspection costs for a single inspection lot or material. These costs are settled on a one-time basis.

Q-69:   A. QM orders by inspection type

The Controlling component uses orders to plan, monitor and settle operating costs. QM orders are the means by which the activities that are performed during quality inspections are linked to account assignment objects in the Controlling component. Once the orders are created, the documented appraisal costs data can be evaluated using three different Quality Costs functions: Display QM Orders by Inspection Type, Display Cost Report for QM Order and Display Cost Report for Inspection Lot Confirmed Activities. In particular, the QM Orders by Inspection Type List refers to all materials for which a QM order has been created that meet selection criteria, such as inspection type, material, plant and QM order. The list, which organizes the orders according to material number, includes material short text, inspection type and inspection type description fields. After the list is created, the user can select an order from the list and display the related material master record or the Controlling data.

Q-70:   B. Rework costs and D. Warranty costs

Efforts made to assure the quality of a product or service result in quality costs. The functions of the Quality Management component lead to the incurrence of two types of quality costs: appraisal costs and nonconformity costs. Nonconformity costs result from the creation of a product or service, the characteristics of which do not conform to defined specifications or standards. Such costs include defect costs, rework costs and warranty costs.

Q-71:   B. Controlling

The Controlling component uses orders to plan, monitor and settle operating costs. QM orders are the means by which the activities that support the processing of quality inspections are linked to account assignment objects in the Controlling component. Like all costs accounted for by the CO component, appraisal costs are classified according to the functional origin of the costs by means of an order category. The functional origin of quality costs is indicated by the order category 06. In turn, standard QM order for appraisal costs order types or custom order types are used to collect the costs that originate with inspection activities.   To account for quality costs, activities are recorded in QM orders in terms of activity types and activity times. The CO component then retrieves predefined prices for the documented activity types and uses the prices to convert the activity times to actual costs. These inspection costs are subsequently settled to cost objects, such as a cost center or a CO internal order, according to account assignments entered when the QM orders were created.   In turn, the system automatically generates offsetting entries to the sender objects, whereas the debit postings remain in place.

Q-72:   A. No account assignment and C. Long-term
cost collector

The Controlling component uses orders to plan,
monitor and settle operating costs. QM orders are the
means by which the activities that are performed during
a quality inspection are linked to account assignment
objects in the Controlling component. Like all costs
accounted for by the Controlling component, an order
category classifies the appraisal costs according to the
functional origin of the costs. The functional origin of
QM quality costs is indicated by the order category 06.
In turn, standard QM order for appraisal costs order
types or custom order types are used to collect the costs
that originate with inspection activities. For example,
the individual QM order for appraisal costs is a short-
term cost collector that's created automatically and used
to collect inspection costs for a single inspection lot or
material. These costs are settled on a one-time basis.

Q-73:   A. Enable the settlement of appraisal costs
that are confirmed in the form of activity times on the
QM order

The Controlling component uses orders to plan,
monitor and settle operating costs. QM orders are the
means by which the activities that support the
processing of quality inspections are linked to account
assignment objects in the Controlling component. Like
all costs accounted for by the CO component, appraisal
and nonconformity costs are classified according to the
functional origin of the costs by means of an order
category. The functional origin of quality costs is

indicated by the order category 06. In turn, standard QM order for appraisal costs order types or custom order types are used to collect the costs that originate with inspection activities. To account for quality costs, activities are recorded in QM orders in terms of activity types and activity times. The CO component then retrieves predefined prices for the documented activity types and uses the prices to convert the activity times to actual costs. These inspection costs are subsequently settled to cost objects, such as a cost center or a CO internal order, according to account assignments entered when the QM orders were created. In turn, the system automatically generates offsetting entries to the sender objects, whereas the debit postings remain in place. Both the Results Recording and the Usage Decision functions can be used to confirm activities for inspection operations.

Q-74:   A. QL01

The Controlling component uses orders to plan, monitor and settle operating costs. QM orders are the means by which the activities that are performed during a quality inspection are linked to account assignment objects in the Controlling component. Like all costs accounted for by the Controlling component, an order category classifies the appraisal costs according to the functional origin of the costs. The functional origin of QM quality costs is indicated by the order category 06. In turn, standard QM order for appraisal costs order types or custom order types are used to collect the costs that originate with inspection activities. The type of QM order used can be determined by the assignment of an order type to the material master record inspection type in Customizing. For example, the general QM order for appraisal costs, QL01, is a long-term cost collector that's created with a manual process and used to collect costs for more than one inspection lot or material. These costs settled periodically. In turn, the individual QM order for appraisal costs, QL02, is a short-term cost collector that's created automatically and used to collect inspection costs for a single inspection lot or material. These costs are settled on a one-time basis.

Q-75:   A. The customer requires a short-term cost collector and B. The customer requires the ability to collect costs on an individual inspection lot basis

The Controlling component uses orders to plan, monitor and settle operating costs. QM orders are the means by which the activities that are performed during a quality inspection are linked to account assignment objects in the Controlling component. Like all costs accounted for by the Controlling component, an order category classifies the appraisal costs according to the functional origin of the costs. The functional origin of QM quality costs is indicated by the order category 06. In turn, standard QM order for appraisal costs order types or custom order types are used to collect the costs that originate with inspection activities. The type of QM order used can be determined by the assignment of an order type to the material master record inspection type in Customizing. For example, the general QM order for appraisal costs, QL01, is a long-term cost collector that's created with a manual process and used

192

to collect costs for more than one inspection lot or material. These costs settled periodically. In turn, the individual QM order for appraisal costs, QL02, is a short-term cost collector that's created automatically and used to collect inspection costs for a single inspection lot or material. These costs are settled on a one-time basis.

Q-76:   C. Change Quality Notification

The Controlling component uses orders to plan, monitor and settle operating costs. The QM order for notifications is the means by which notification processing activities are linked to cost assignment objects in the Controlling component. Like all costs accounted for by the Controlling component, notification costs are classified according to the functional origin of the costs by means of an order category. The functional origin of quality costs is represented by the order category 06. In turn, a new or existing QM order for nonconformity costs order type, QN03, is created manually and used to collect notification processing costs. Each activity performed to process the notification is recorded in terms of an activity type and activity time. The CO component then identifies the predefined price associated with the activity type for which the activity times were recorded in QM and converts the activity times to an actual cost on the basis of the predefined prices stored in the CO component. The nonconformity costs are then settled to one or more cost objects, such as a cost center or controlling area, according to the account assignment that is entered when the QM order for non-conformity costs was created. The system automatically generates offsetting entries to the sender objects, whereas the debit postings to sender objects remain in place. The Change Quality Notification function is used to create a QM order for nonconformity costs and assign it to the notification.

Q-77:   A. Activity types and C. Activity times

The Controlling component uses orders to plan, monitor and settle operating costs. QM orders are the means by which the activities that support the processing of quality inspections are linked to account assignment objects in the Controlling component. Like all costs accounted for by the CO component, appraisal and nonconformity costs are classified according to the functional origin of the costs by means of an order category. The functional origin of quality costs is indicated by the order category 06. In turn, standard QM order for appraisal costs order types or custom order types are used to collect the costs that originate with inspection activities.   To account for quality costs, activities are recorded in QM orders in terms of activity types and activity times. The CO component then retrieves predefined prices for the documented activity types and uses the prices to convert the activity times to actual costs. These inspection costs are subsequently settled to cost objects, such as a cost center or a CO internal order, according to account assignments entered when the QM orders were created. In turn, the system automatically generates offsetting entries to the sender objects, whereas the debit postings remain in place.

Q-78:   B. Individual QM order for appraisal costs

The Controlling component uses orders to plan, monitor and settle operating costs. QM orders are the means by which the activities that are performed during a quality inspection are linked to account assignment objects in the Controlling component. Like all costs accounted for by the Controlling component, an order category classifies the appraisal costs according to the functional origin of the costs. The functional origin of QM quality costs is indicated by the order category 06. In turn, standard QM order for appraisal costs order types or custom order types are used to collect the costs that originate with inspection activities. The type of QM order used can be determined by the assignment of an order type to the material master record inspection type in Customizing. For example, the general QM order for appraisal costs, QL01, is a long-term cost collector that's created with a manual process and used to collect costs for more than one inspection lot or material. These costs settled periodically. In turn, the individual QM order for appraisal costs, QL02, is a short-term cost collector that's created automatically and used to collect inspection costs for a single inspection lot or material. These costs are settled on a one-time basis.

Q-79:   A. Individual QM order

The Controlling component uses orders to plan, monitor and settle operating costs. QM orders are the means by which the activities that are performed during a quality inspection are linked to account assignment objects in the Controlling component. Like all costs accounted for by the Controlling component, an order category classifies the appraisal costs according to the functional origin of the costs. The functional origin of QM quality costs is indicated by the order category 06. In turn, standard QM order for appraisal costs order types or custom order types are used to collect the costs that originate with inspection activities. The type of QM order used can be determined by the assignment of an order type to the material master record inspection type in Customizing. For example, the general QM order for appraisal costs, QL01, is a long-term cost collector that's created with a manual process and used to collect costs for more than one inspection lot or material. These costs settled periodically. In turn, the individual QM order for appraisal costs, QL02, is a short-term cost collector that's created automatically and used to collect inspection costs for a single inspection lot or material. These costs are settled on a one-time basis.

Q-80:   A. Plant and B. Material

The Controlling component uses orders to plan, monitor and settle operating costs. QM orders are the means by which the activities that support the processing of quality inspections are linked to account assignment objects in the Controlling component. Like all costs accounted for by the Controlling component, QM costs are classified according to the functional origin of the costs by means of an order category. The functional origin of quality costs is indicated by the order category 06. In turn, either standard QM order

196

types or custom order types are used to collect QM costs. The creation and assignment of a general or individual QM order with the central maintenance function requires the entry of selection criteria including plant, inspection type and/or material. After the order is created, activity costs can be recorded. To account for QM costs, activities are recorded in QM orders in terms of activity types and activity times. The CO component then retrieves predefined prices for the documented activity types and uses the prices to convert the activity times to actual costs. The costs are subsequently settled to cost objects, such as a cost center or a CO internal order, according to account assignments entered when the QM orders were created.

Q-81:   A. Assignment of work center to cost center in PP and C. Assignment of work center to operation in inspection plan in QM

The Controlling component uses orders to plan, monitor and settle operating costs. QM orders are the means by which the activities that support the processing of quality inspections are linked to account assignment objects in the Controlling component. Like all costs accounted for by the Controlling component, an order category classifies the appraisal costs according to the functional origin of the costs. The functional origin of quality costs is indicated by the order category 06. In turn, standard QM order for appraisal costs order types or custom order types are used to collect the costs that originate with inspection activities. These activities are recorded in orders in terms of activity types and activity times. The CO component then retrieves predefined prices for the documented activity types and uses the prices to convert the activity times to actual costs.   The inspection costs are then settled to cost objects according to account assignments entered when the QM orders were created.   In turn, the system automatically generates offsetting entries to the sender objects, whereas the debit postings remain in place.

Q-82:   D. Settlement of the actual costs for the QM order

The Controlling component uses orders to plan, monitor and settle operating costs. QM orders are the means by which the activities that support the processing of quality inspections are linked to account assignment objects in the Controlling component. Like all costs accounted for by the Controlling component, an order category classifies the appraisal costs according to the functional origin of the costs. The functional origin of quality costs is indicated by the order category 06. In turn, standard QM order for appraisal costs order types or custom order types are used to collect the costs that originate with inspection activities. These activities are recorded in orders in terms of activity types and activity times. The CO component then retrieves predefined prices for the documented activity types and uses the prices to convert the activity times to actual costs.   The inspection costs are then settled to cost objects according to account assignments entered when the QM orders were created.   In turn, the system automatically generates offsetting entries to the sender objects, whereas the debit postings remain in place.

Q-83:   C. Activity types

The Controlling component uses orders to plan, monitor and settle operating costs. QM orders are the means by which the activities that support the processing of quality inspections are linked to account assignment objects in the Controlling component. Like all costs accounted for by the Controlling component, an order category classifies the appraisal costs according to the functional origin of the costs. The functional origin of quality costs is indicated by the order category 06. In turn, standard QM order for appraisal costs order types or custom order types are used to collect the costs that originate with inspection activities. These activities are recorded in orders in terms of activity types and activity times. The CO component then retrieves predefined prices for the documented activity types and uses the prices to convert the activity times to actual costs. The inspection costs are then settled to cost objects according to account assignments entered when the QM orders were created. In turn, the system automatically generates offsetting entries to the sender objects, whereas the debit postings remain in place.

Q-84:   A. Incorrect work center entered when inspection results are recorded and B. Incorrect plant entered when inspection results are recorded

The Controlling component uses orders to plan, monitor and settle operating costs. QM orders are the means by which the activities that support the processing of quality inspections are linked to account assignment objects in the Controlling component. Like all costs accounted for by the Controlling component, QM costs are classified according to the functional origin of the costs by means of an order category. The functional origin of quality costs is indicated by the order category 06. In turn, either standard QM order types or a custom order type are used to collect QM costs. To account for QM costs, activities are recorded in QM orders in terms of activity types and activity times. The CO component then retrieves predefined prices for the documented activity types and uses the prices to convert the activity times to actual costs. The costs are subsequently settled to cost objects, such as a cost center or a CO internal order, according to account assignments entered when the QM orders were created. The confirmation of activities for quality inspection operations during the Results Recording process requires the entry of a work center and plant. Optional entries include setup time, machine time and labor.

Q-85:   B. Enter set-up time and C. Enter labor time

The Controlling component uses orders to plan, monitor and settle operating costs. QM orders are the means by which the activities that support the processing of quality inspections are linked to account assignment objects in the Controlling component. Like all costs accounted for by the Controlling component, an order category classifies the appraisal costs according to the functional origin of the costs. The functional origin of quality costs is indicated by the order category 06. In turn, the standard QM order for appraisal costs order types or custom order types are used to collect the costs that originate with inspection activities. Inspection activities are recorded in orders in terms of activity, such as set-up types, and activity times. To confirm activities during the results recording process requires the entry of the work center and plant. The CO component then retrieves predefined prices for the documented activity types and uses the prices to convert the activity times to actual costs. These inspection costs are then settled to cost objects according to account assignments entered when the QM orders were created. The entry of set-up time or labor time is not a required step to confirm activities during the results recording process.

Q-86:   C. Multiple selection function in Create QM Order function

The Controlling component uses orders to plan, monitor and settle operating costs. QM orders are the means by which the activities that support the processing of quality inspections are linked to account assignment objects in the Controlling component. Like all costs accounted for by the Controlling component, an order category classifies the appraisal costs according to the functional origin of the costs. The functional origin of quality costs is indicated by the order category 06. In turn, the QM order for inspection costs order types are used to collect the costs that originate with inspection activities. The QM order is created and inspection costs are collected on the basis of plant, inspection type and or material. As the order is created, the multiple selection function can be used to select inspection data on the basis of multiple inspection types or materials. This data is recorded in orders in terms of activity types and activity times. The CO component then retrieves predefined prices for the documented activity types and uses the prices to convert the activity times to actual costs. These inspection costs are then settled to cost objects according to account assignments entered when the QM orders were created. In turn, the system automatically generates offsetting entries to the sender objects, whereas the debit postings remain in place.

Q-87: B. Summarize costs for all materials or inspection lots associated with a general order for appraisal costs

The Controlling component uses orders to plan, monitor and settle operating costs. QM orders are the means by which the activities that are performed during quality inspections are linked to account assignment objects in the Controlling component. Once the orders are created, the documented appraisal costs data can be evaluated using three different Quality Costs functions: Display QM Orders by Inspection Type, Display Cost Report for QM Order and Display Cost Report for Inspection Lot Confirmed Activities. In particular, the Cost Report for a General QM Order summarizes costs for all inspection lots associated with a particular general QM order for inspection costs.

The report , which organizes the orders according to cost element, such as machine time or labor time, includes the activity times and confirmed costs for each costs element. The user can display the report as a graphic and export the report to another application, such as Excel.

Q-88:   B. Costs incurred to inspect the quality of a product or material and C. Costs incurred due to the failure to maintain acceptable quality levels

Efforts made to assure the quality of a product or service result in quality costs. The functions of the Quality Management component lead to the incurrence of two types of quality costs: appraisal costs and nonconformity costs. Nonconformity costs result from the creation of a product or service, the characteristics of which do not conform to defined specifications or standards. Such costs include defect costs, rework costs and warranty costs. In turn, appraisal costs result from the performance of inspections that confirm the quality of products and the conformance of the products to established benchmarks. Such costs include labor, material and equipment costs.
Efforts made to assure the quality of a product or service result in quality costs. The functions of the Quality Management component lead to the incurrence of two types of quality costs: appraisal costs and nonconformity costs. Nonconformity costs result from the creation of a product or service, the characteristics of which do not conform to defined specifications or standards. Such costs include defect costs, rework costs and warranty costs. In turn, appraisal costs result

from the performance of inspections that confirm the quality of products and the conformance of the products to established benchmarks. Such costs include labor, material and equipment costs.

Q-89:   B. Account assignment for the order is specified

The Controlling component uses orders to plan, monitor and settle operating costs. QM orders are the means by which activities that are performed to process a notification are linked to cost assignment objects in the Controlling component. As with all costs accounted for by the Controlling component, an order category is used to classify notification costs according to the functional origin of the costs. The order category for quality notifications is 06. In turn, a new or existing standard QM order for nonconformity costs is used to collect costs that originate with notification activities. The QM order type for notifications is QN01. To account for nonconformity costs using the QM order QN01, the order is created manually and assigned to the notification header as the notification is processed. As the notification is processed, the activities are recorded in the QM order in terms of activity types and activity times. The CO component then retrieves predefined prices for the documented activity types and uses the prices to convert the activity times to actual costs. These nonconformity costs that are incurred to process the notification are then settled to one or more cost objects, such as a cost center or a CO internal order, according to the account assignment that is entered when the QM order was created. When the nonconformity costs are settled to cost objects, the system automatically generates offsetting entries to the sender objects whereas the debit postings remain in place.

Q-90:   B. Order type

The Controlling component uses orders to plan, monitor and settle operating costs. QM orders are the means by which the activities that support the processing of quality inspections and notifications are linked to cost assignment objects in the Controlling component. Like all costs accounted for by the Controlling component, Like all costs accounted for by the CO component, appraisal and nonconformity costs are classified according to the functional origin of the costs by means of an order category. The functional origin of quality costs is indicated by the order category 06. In turn, either the QM order for inspection costs order types, QL01 and QL02, or custom order types are used to collect costs that originate with the inspection activities. In turn, the QM order type for nonconformity costs, QN03, or a custom order type is used to collect costs that originate with notification-processing activities.

Q-91:   C: QN03

The Controlling component uses orders to plan, monitor and settle operating costs. QM orders are the means by which the activities that support the processing of quality inspections and notifications are linked to cost assignment objects in the Controlling component. Like all costs accounted for by the

Controlling component, Like all costs accounted for by the CO component, appraisal and nonconformity costs are classified according to the functional origin of the costs by means of an order category. The functional origin of quality costs is indicated by the order category 06. In turn, either the QM order for inspection costs order types, QL01 and QL02, or custom order types are used to collect costs that originate with the inspection activities. In turn, the QM order type for nonconformity costs, QN03, or a custom order type is used to collect costs that originate with notification-processing activities.

Q-92:   A. The customer requires that the order type be a long-term cost collector and C. The customer requires the ability to settle costs in CO on a monthly basis

The Controlling component uses orders to plan, monitor and settle operating costs. QM orders are the means by which the activities that are performed during a quality inspection are linked to account assignment objects in the Controlling component. Like all costs accounted for by the Controlling component, an order category classifies the appraisal costs according to the functional origin of the costs. The functional origin of QM quality costs is indicated by the order category 06. In turn, standard QM order for appraisal costs order types or custom order types are used to collect the costs that originate with inspection activities. The type of QM order used can be determined by the assignment of an order type to the material master record inspection type in Customizing. For example, the general QM

order for appraisal costs, QL01, is a long-term cost collector that's created with a manual process and used to collect costs for more than one inspection lot or material. These costs settled periodically. In turn, the individual QM order for appraisal costs, QL02, is a short-term cost collector that's created automatically and used to collect inspection costs for a single inspection lot or material. These costs are settled on a one-time basis.

Q-93:   B. QM order type QL02

The Controlling component uses orders to plan, monitor and settle operating costs. QM orders are the means by which the activities that are performed during a quality inspection are linked to account assignment objects in the Controlling component. Like all costs accounted for by the Controlling component, an order category classifies the appraisal costs according to the functional origin of the costs. The functional origin of QM quality costs is indicated by the order category 06. In turn, standard QM order for appraisal costs order types or custom order types are used to collect the costs that originate with inspection activities. The type of QM order used can be determined by the assignment of an order type to the material master record inspection type in Customizing. For example, the general QM order for appraisal costs, QL01, is a long-term cost collector that's created with a manual process and used to collect costs for more than one inspection lot or material. These costs settled periodically. In turn, the individual QM order for appraisal costs, QL02, is a short-term cost collector that's created automatically and used to collect inspection costs for a single inspection lot or material. These costs are settled on a one-time basis.

Q-94:   A. Incorrect settlement receiver is entered in QM order

The Controlling component uses orders to plan, monitor and settle operating costs. QM orders are the means by which the activities that are performed during a quality inspection are linked to cost assignment objects in the Controlling component. Like all costs accounted for by the Controlling component, an order category classifies the appraisal costs according to the functional origin of the costs. The functional origin of QM quality costs is indicated by the order category 06. In turn, standard QM order for appraisal costs order types or custom order types are used to collect the costs that originate with inspection activities. For example, the general QM order for appraisal costs is a long-term cost collector that's created with a manual process and used to collect costs for more than one inspection lot or material. These costs are settled periodically. In turn, the individual QM order for appraisal costs is a short-term cost collector used to collect inspection costs for a single inspection lot or material. These costs are settled on a one-time basis. To account for appraisal costs using an individual QM order for appraisal costs, the order is created as the inspection lot is created. The order is then assigned to the inspection lot. Following the inspection, inspection activities are recorded in the QM order in terms of activity types that are defined for a work center and related activity times as characteristic inspection results are recorded and valuated or as the usage decision for the inspection lot is documented. The CO component then retrieves predefined prices for the documented activity types and uses the prices to convert the activity times to actual costs. These appraisal costs are settled to a cost object, such as a cost center or a CO internal order, according to a settlement rule that's defined for the QM order master record. In turn, settlement profiles, which are defined in Customizing, determine the allowed receiver for each order type. For example, the standard settlement receiver control indicator is set in the order if a single settlement of costs to a cost center or CO internal order is desired. The special settlement rule control indicator is set if a distribution rule is used to settle costs to several receivers. When appraisal costs are settled to cost objects, the system generates offsetting entries to the sender objects, whereas the debit postings remain in place.

Q-95:   A. Create QM Order

The Controlling component uses orders to plan, monitor and settle operating costs. QM orders are the means by which the activities that support the processing of quality inspections are linked to account assignment objects in the Controlling component. Like all costs accounted for by the Controlling component, an order category classifies the appraisal costs according to the functional origin of the costs. The functional origin of quality costs is indicated by the order category 06. In turn, the QM order for inspection costs order types are used to collect the costs that originate with inspection activities. The QM order is created and inspection costs are collected on the basis of plant, inspection type and or material. As the order is created, the multiple selection function can be used to select inspection data on the basis of multiple inspection types or materials. This data is recorded in orders in terms of activity types and activity times. The CO component then retrieves predefined prices for the documented activity types and uses the prices to convert the activity times to actual costs. These inspection costs are then settled to cost objects according to account assignments entered when the QM orders were created. In turn, the system automatically generates offsetting entries to the sender objects, whereas the debit postings remain in place. Create/Copy/Replace QM Order, Results Recording: Confirm Activities, Usage Decision: Confirm Activities and Define Report variant are functions that support the collection of appraisal costs during a quality inspection.

Q-96: A. Plant and B. Material

The Controlling component uses orders to plan, monitor and settle operating costs. QM orders are the means by which the activities that support the processing of quality inspections are linked to account assignment objects in the Controlling component. Like all costs accounted for by the Controlling component, an order category classifies the appraisal costs according to the functional origin of the costs. The functional origin of quality costs is indicated by the order category 06. In turn, standard QM order for appraisal costs order types or custom order types are used to collect the costs that originate with inspection activities. For example, the individual QM order for appraisal costs is a short-term cost collector used to document the actual appraisal costs incurred to process a single inspection lot, which are settled on a one-time basis. Using this order type, activities are selected on the basis of plant, inspection type and/or material and recorded in terms of activity types and activity times in the order. The CO component retrieves predefined prices for the documented activity types and uses the prices to convert the activity times to actual costs. These inspection costs are settled to cost objects according to account assignments entered when the QM orders were created. In turn, the system automatically generates offsetting entries to the sender objects, whereas the debit postings remain in place.

Q-97:   B. Inspection type and C. Material class

The Controlling component uses orders to plan, monitor and settle operating costs. QM orders are the means by which the activities that support the processing of quality inspections are linked to account assignment objects in the Controlling component. Like all costs accounted for by the Controlling component, an order category classifies the appraisal costs according to the functional origin of the costs. The functional origin of quality costs is indicated by the order category 06. In turn, standard QM order for appraisal costs order types or custom order types are used to collect the costs that originate with inspection activities. For example, the individual QM order for appraisal costs is a short-term cost collector used to document the actual appraisal costs incurred to process a single inspection lot, which are settled on a one-time basis. Using this order type, activities are selected on the basis of plant, inspection type and/or material and recorded in terms of activity types and activity times in the order. The CO component retrieves predefined prices for the documented activity types and uses the prices to convert the activity times to actual costs. These inspection costs are settled to cost objects according to account assignments entered when the QM orders were created. In turn, the system automatically generates offsetting entries to the sender objects, whereas the debit postings remain in place.

Q-98:   C. Assign work center to operation in plan and E. Define standard values for activity types in operation

The Controlling component uses orders to plan, monitor and settle operating costs. QM orders are the means by which the activities that are performed during a quality inspection are linked to account assignment objects in the Controlling component. Like all costs accounted for by the Controlling component, an order category classifies the appraisal costs according to the functional origin of the costs. The functional origin of QM quality costs is indicated by the order category 06. In turn, standard QM order for appraisal costs order types or custom order types are used to collect the costs that originate with inspection activities. The type of QM order used can be determined by the assignment of an order type to the material master record inspection type in Customizing. For example, the general QM

order for appraisal costs is a long-term cost collector that's created with a manual process and used to collect costs for more than one inspection lot or material. These costs settled periodically. In turn, the individual QM order for appraisal costs is a short-term cost collector that's created automatically and used to collect inspection costs for a single inspection lot or material. These costs are settled on a one-time basis. To account for appraisal costs using an individual QM order for appraisal costs, the order is created as the inspection lot is created. The order is then assigned to the inspection lot. Following the inspection, inspection activities are recorded in the QM order in terms of activity types that are defined for a work center and related activity times as characteristic inspection results are recorded and valuated or as the usage decision for the inspection lot is documented. Next, the CO component retrieves predefined prices for the documented activity types and uses the prices to convert the activity times to actual costs. These appraisal costs are settled to a cost object, such as a cost center or a CO internal order, according to a settlement rule that's defined for the QM order master record. In turn, settlement profiles, which are defined in Customizing, determine the allowed receiver for each order type. When the appraisal costs are settled to cost objects, the system generates offsetting entries to the sender objects, whereas the debit postings remain in place. The confirmation of activities for quality inspection operations requires the creation of activity types for work centers and activity prices in Controlling and the assignment of work centers to cost objects in PP. Activity confirmation also requires the assignment of a work center to a plan operation, the

213

definition of standard values for activity types and the assignment of the QM order to the inspection lot in QM. Also needed is the assignment of a QM order to the inspection lot and the use of an inspection plan for the inspection.

Q-99:   B. Activity types are defined for each work center

The Controlling component uses orders to plan, monitor and settle operating costs. QM orders are the means by which the activities that are performed during a quality inspection are linked to account assignment objects in the Controlling component. Like all costs accounted for by the Controlling component, an order category classifies the appraisal costs according to the functional origin of the costs. The functional origin of QM quality costs is indicated by the order category 06. In turn, standard QM order for appraisal costs order types or custom order types are used to collect the costs that originate with inspection activities. The type of QM order used can be determined by the assignment of an order type to the material master record inspection type in Customizing. For example, the general QM order for appraisal costs is a long-term cost collector that's created with a manual process and used to collect costs for more than one inspection lot or material. These costs settled periodically. In turn, the individual QM order for appraisal costs is a short-term cost collector that's created automatically and used to collect inspection costs for a single inspection lot or material. These costs are settled on a one-time basis. To account for appraisal costs using an individual QM order for appraisal costs, the order is created as the inspection lot is created. The order is then assigned to the inspection lot. Following the inspection, inspection activities are recorded in the QM order in terms of activity types that are defined for a work center and related activity times as characteristic inspection results are recorded and valuated or as the usage decision for the inspection lot is documented. Next, the CO component retrieves predefined prices for the documented activity types and uses the prices to convert the activity times to actual costs. These appraisal costs are settled to a cost object, such as a cost center or a CO internal order, according to a settlement rule that's defined for the QM order master record. In turn, settlement profiles, which are defined in Customizing, determine the allowed receiver for each order type. When the appraisal costs are settled to cost objects, the system generates offsetting entries to the sender objects, whereas the debit postings remain in place. The confirmation of activities for quality inspection operations requires the creation of activity types for work centers and activity prices in Controlling and the assignment of work centers to cost objects in PP. Activity confirmation also requires the assignment of a work center to a plan operation, the definition of standard values for activity types and the assignment of the QM order to the inspection lot in QM. Also needed is the assignment of a QM order to the inspection lot and the use of an inspection plan for the inspection.

Q-100:   C. Confirmation required control indicator for the inspection operation

The Controlling component uses orders to plan, monitor and settle operating costs. QM orders are the means by which the activities that are performed during a quality inspection are linked to account assignment objects in the Controlling component. Like all costs accounted for by the Controlling component, an order category classifies the appraisal costs according to the functional origin of the costs. The functional origin of QM quality costs is indicated by the order category 06. In turn, standard QM order for appraisal costs order types or custom order types are used to collect the costs that originate with inspection activities. The type of QM order used can be determined by the assignment of an order type to the material master record inspection type in Customizing. For example, the general QM order for appraisal costs is a long-term cost collector that's created with a manual process and used to collect costs for more than one inspection lot or material. These costs settled periodically. In turn, the individual QM order for appraisal costs is a short-term cost collector that's created automatically and used to collect inspection costs for a single inspection lot or material. These costs are settled on a one-time basis. To account for appraisal costs using an individual QM order for appraisal costs, the order is created as the inspection lot is created. The order is then assigned to the inspection lot. Following the inspection, inspection activities are recorded in the QM order in terms of activity types that are defined for a work center and related activity times as characteristic inspection results are recorded and valuated or as the usage decision for the inspection lot is documented. Next, the CO component retrieves predefined prices for the documented activity types and uses the prices to convert the activity times to actual costs. These appraisal costs are settled to a cost object, such as a cost center or a CO internal order, according to a settlement rule that's defined for the QM order master record. In turn, settlement profiles, which are defined in Customizing, determine the allowed receiver for each order type. When the appraisal costs are settled to cost objects, the system generates offsetting entries to the sender objects, whereas the debit postings remain in place. The confirmation of activities for quality inspection operations requires the creation of activity types for work centers and activity prices in Controlling and the assignment of work centers to cost objects in PP. Activity confirmation also requires the assignment of a work center to a plan operation, the definition of standard values for activity types and the assignment of the QM order to the inspection lot in QM. Also needed is the assignment of a QM order to the inspection lot and the use of an inspection plan for the inspection.

Q-101:   A. QM order by inspection type

The Controlling component uses orders to plan, monitor and settle operating costs. QM orders are the means by which the activities that are performed during quality inspections are linked to account assignment objects in the Controlling component. Once the orders are created, the documented appraisal costs data can be evaluated using three different Quality Costs functions: Display QM Orders by Inspection Type, Display Cost Report for QM Order and Display Cost Report for Inspection Lot Confirmed Activities. In particular, the

QM Orders by Inspection Type List refers to all materials for which a QM order has been created that meet selection criteria, such as inspection type, material, plant and QM order. The list, which organizes the orders according to material number, includes material short text, inspection type and inspection type description fields. After the list is created, the user can select an order from the list and display the related material master record or the Controlling data.

Q-102:   A. Controlling

The Controlling component uses orders to plan, monitor and settle operating costs. QM orders are the means by which the activities that support the processing of quality inspections are linked to account assignment objects in the Controlling component. Like all costs accounted for by the Controlling component, an order category classifies the appraisal costs according to the functional origin of the costs. The functional origin of quality costs is indicated by the order category 06. In turn, the QM order for inspection costs order types are used to collect the costs that originate with inspection activities. These activities are recorded in orders in terms of activity types and activity times. The CO component then retrieves predefined prices for the documented activity types and uses the prices to convert the activity times to actual costs. These inspection costs are then settled to cost objects according to account assignments entered when the QM orders were created. In turn, the system automatically generates offsetting entries to the sender objects and the debit postings to the objects remain in place. The automatic confirmation of activities during the results recording process requires the selection of the confirmation indicator for the inspection operation.

Q-103:   C. Work center assigned to inspection operation

The Controlling component uses orders to plan, monitor and settle operating costs. QM orders are the means by which the activities that support the processing of quality inspections are linked to account assignment objects in the Controlling component. Like all costs accounted for by the Controlling component, an order category classifies the appraisal costs according to the functional origin of the costs. The functional origin of quality costs is indicated by the order category 06. In turn, standard QM order for appraisal costs order types or custom order types are used to collect the costs that originate with inspection activities. For example, the general QM order for appraisal costs is a long-term cost collector used to collect costs for more than one inspection lot or material and the individual QM order for appraisal costs is a short-term cost collector used to collect inspection costs for a single inspection lot or material. To account for appraisal costs, inspection activities are recorded in QM orders in terms of activity types and activity times as inspection results are recorded or the usage decision for the inspection lot is documented. The CO component then retrieves predefined prices for the documented activity types and uses the prices to convert the activity times to actual costs. These inspection costs are subsequently settled to cost objects, such as a cost center or a CO internal order, according to account assignments entered when the QM orders were created. In turn, the system automatically generates offsetting entries to the sender objects, whereas the debit postings remain in place. The confirmation of activities for quality inspection operations requires the creation of activity types for work centers and activity prices in Controlling, the assignment of work centers to cost objects in PP, the assignment of work centers to a plan operation, the definition of standard values for activity types for operations, and the assignment of the QM order to the inspection lot in QM.

Q-104:   A. Activity type

The Controlling component uses orders to plan, monitor and settle operating costs. QM orders are the means by which the activities that are performed during a quality inspection are linked to account assignment objects in the Controlling component. Like all costs accounted for by the Controlling component, an order category classifies the appraisal costs according to the functional origin of the costs. The functional origin of QM quality costs is indicated by the order category 06. In turn, standard QM order for appraisal costs order types or custom order types are used to collect the costs that originate with inspection activities. The type of QM order used can be determined by the assignment of an order type to the material master record inspection type in Customizing. For example, the individual QM order for appraisal costs is a short-term cost collector that's created automatically and used to collect inspection costs for a single inspection lot or material.

These costs are settled on a one-time basis. To account for appraisal costs using an individual QM order for appraisal costs, the order is created as the inspection lot is created. The order is then assigned to the inspection lot. Following the inspection, inspection activities are recorded in the QM order in terms of activity types that are defined for a work center and related activity times as characteristic inspection results are recorded and valuated, or as the usage decision for the inspection lot is documented. Next, the CO component retrieves predefined prices for the documented activity types and uses the prices to convert the activity times to actual costs. These appraisal costs are settled to a cost object, such as a cost center or a CO internal order, according to a settlement rule that's defined for the QM order master record. In turn, settlement profiles, which are defined in Customizing, determine the allowed receiver for each order type. When the appraisal costs are settled to cost objects, the system generates offsetting entries to the sender objects, whereas the debit postings remain in place.

Q-105:   B. Display cost report for QM order

The Controlling component uses orders to plan, monitor and settle operating costs. QM orders are the means by which the activities that are performed during quality inspections are linked to account assignment objects in the Controlling component. Once the orders are created, the documented appraisal costs data can be evaluated using three different Quality Costs functions: Display QM Orders by Inspection Type, Display Cost Report for QM Order and Display Cost Report for

Inspection Lot Confirmed Activities. In particular, the Display Cost Report for QM Order refers to summarized costs for all materials or inspection lots assigned to an individual or general QM order. The report organizes activity types and costs according to individual cost elements. The user can display the data in a list or as a graph. Also, the cost data can be exported the to an Excel spreadsheet or printed.

Q-106:   D. Costs incurred due to the failure to maintain an acceptable quality level of a product or material are recorded

Efforts made to assure the quality of a product or service result in quality costs. The functions of the Quality Management component lead to the incurrence of two types of quality costs: appraisal costs and nonconformity costs. Nonconformity costs result from the creation of a product or service, the characteristics of which do not conform to defined specifications or standards. Nonconformity costs include the costs of analyzing product and material defects and the completion of activities, which rectify issues that affect product quality. Such costs include defect costs, rework costs and warranty costs.

Q-107:   B. Order category 06 and E. Order type QN01

The Controlling component uses orders to plan, monitor and settle operating costs. QM orders are the means by which the activities that are performed during a quality inspection are linked to account assignment objects in the Controlling component. Like all costs accounted for by the Controlling component, an order category classifies the appraisal costs according to the functional origin of the costs. The functional origin of QM quality costs is indicated by the order category 06. In turn, standard QM order for appraisal costs order types or custom order types are used to collect the costs that originate with inspection activities. The type of QM order used can be determined by the assignment of an order type to the material master record inspection type in Customizing. For example, the general QM order for appraisal costs, QL01, is a long-term cost collector that's created with a manual process and used to collect costs for more than one inspection lot or material. These costs settled periodically. In turn, the individual QM order for appraisal costs, QL02, is a short-term cost collector that's created automatically and used to collect inspection costs for a single inspection lot or material. These costs are settled on a one-time basis. The QM order type for nonconformity costs, QN01, is used to collect costs that originate with notification-processing activities.

Q-108:   B. Cost Report for QM Order

The Controlling component uses orders to plan, monitor and settle operating costs. QM orders are the means by which the activities that are performed during quality inspections are linked to account assignment objects in the Controlling component. Once the orders are created, the documented appraisal costs data can be evaluated using three different Quality Costs functions: Display QM Orders by Inspection Type, Display Cost Report for QM Order and Display Cost Report for

Inspection Lot Confirmed Activities. In particular, the Display Cost Report for QM Order refers to summarized costs for the materials or inspection lots assigned to a general or individual QM order. The report organizes the activity types and costs according to individual cost elements. The user can display the data in the list as a graph or export the cost data to an Excel spreadsheet. The report can also be printed.

Q-109:   A. Assignment of QM order to an inspection lot

The Controlling component uses orders to plan, monitor and settle operating costs. QM orders are the means by which the activities that support the processing of quality inspections are linked to account assignment objects in the Controlling component. Like all costs accounted for by the Controlling component, an order category classifies the appraisal costs according to the functional origin of the costs. The functional origin of quality costs is indicated by the order category 06. In turn, standard QM order for appraisal costs order types or custom order types are used to collect the costs that originate with inspection activities. For example, the general QM order for appraisal costs is a long-term cost collector used to collect costs for more than one inspection lot or material and the individual QM order for appraisal costs is a short-term cost collector used to collect inspection costs for a single inspection lot or material. To account for appraisal costs, inspection activities are recorded in QM orders in terms of activity types and activity times as inspection results are recorded or the usage decision for the inspection lot is documented. The CO component then retrieves predefined prices for the documented activity types and uses the prices to convert the activity times to actual costs. These inspection costs are subsequently settled to cost objects, such as a cost center or a CO internal order, according to account assignments entered when the QM orders were created. In turn, the system automatically generates offsetting entries to the sender objects, whereas the debit postings remain in place. The confirmation of activities for quality inspection operations requires the creation of activity types for work centers and activity prices in Controlling, the assignment of work centers to cost objects in PP, the assignment of work centers to a plan operation, the definition of standard values for activity types for operations, and the assignment of the QM order to the inspection lot in QM.

Q-110:   A. The term for which the order collects inspection costs

The Controlling component uses orders to plan, monitor and settle operating costs. QM orders are the means by which the activities that are performed during a quality inspection are linked to cost assignment objects in the Controlling component. Like all costs accounted for by the Controlling component, an order category classifies the appraisal costs according to the functional origin of the costs. The functional origin of QM quality costs is indicated by the order category 06. In turn, standard QM order for appraisal costs order types or custom order types are used to collect the costs that originate with inspection activities. For example, the general QM order for appraisal costs is a long-term cost collector that's created with a manual process and used to collect costs for more than one inspection lot or material. These costs are settled periodically. In turn, the individual QM order for appraisal costs is a short-term cost collector used to collect inspection costs for a single inspection lot or material. These costs are settled on a one-time basis. To account for appraisal costs using an individual QM order for appraisal costs, the order is created as the inspection lot is created. The order is then assigned to the inspection lot. Following the inspection, inspection activities are recorded in the QM order in terms of activity types that are defined for a work center and related activity times as characteristic inspection results are recorded and valuated or as the usage decision for the inspection lot is documented. The CO component then retrieves predefined prices for the documented activity types and uses the prices to convert the activity times to actual costs. These appraisal costs are settled to a cost object, such as a cost center or a CO internal order, according to a settlement rule that's defined for the QM order master record. In turn, settlement profiles, which are defined in Customizing, determine the allowed receiver for each order type. For example, the standard settlement receiver control indicator is set in the order if a single settlement of costs to a cost center or CO internal order is desired. The special settlement rule control indicator is set if a distribution rule is used to settle costs to several receivers. When the appraisal costs are settled to cost objects, the system generates offsetting entries to the sender objects, whereas the debit postings remain in place.

Q-111:   B. QL02

The Controlling component uses orders to plan, monitor and settle operating costs. QM orders are the means by which the activities that are performed during a quality inspection are linked to account assignment objects in the Controlling component. Like all costs accounted for by the Controlling component, an order category classifies the appraisal costs according to the functional origin of the costs. The functional origin of QM quality costs is indicated by the order category 06. In turn, standard QM order for appraisal costs order types or custom order types are used to collect the costs that originate with inspection activities. The type of QM order used can be determined by the assignment of an order type to the material master record inspection type in Customizing.   For example, the general QM order for appraisal costs, QL01, is a long-term cost collector that's created with a manual process and used to collect costs for more than one inspection lot or material. These costs settled periodically. In turn, the individual QM order for appraisal costs, QL02, is a short-term cost collector that's created automatically and used to collect inspection costs for a single inspection lot or material. These costs are settled on a one-time basis. The QM order type for nonconformity costs, QN01, is used to collect costs that originate with notification-processing activities.

Q-112:   A. Material master record

The Controlling component uses orders to plan, monitor and settle operating costs. QM orders are the means by which the activities that are performed during a quality inspection are linked to cost assignment objects in the Controlling component. Like all costs accounted for by the Controlling component, an order category classifies the appraisal costs according to the functional origin of the costs. The functional origin of QM quality costs is indicated by the order category 06. In turn, standard QM order for appraisal costs order types or custom order types are used to collect the costs that originate with inspection activities. For example, the general QM order for appraisal costs is a long-term cost collector that's created with a manual process and used to collect costs for more than one inspection lot or material. These costs are settled periodically. In turn, the individual QM order for appraisal costs is a short-term cost collector used to collect inspection costs for a single inspection lot or material. These costs are settled on a one-time basis. The type of QM order used is determined by the assignment of the order type to the material master record inspection type. To account for appraisal costs using an individual QM order for appraisal costs, the order is created as the inspection lot is created. The order is then assigned to the inspection lot. Following the inspection, inspection activities are recorded in the QM order in terms of activity types that are defined for a work center and related activity times as characteristic inspection results are recorded and valuated or as the usage decision for the inspection lot is documented. The CO component then retrieves predefined prices for the documented activity types and uses the prices to convert the activity times to actual costs. These appraisal costs are settled to a cost object, such as a cost center or a CO internal order, according to a settlement rule that's defined for the QM order master record. In turn, settlement profiles, which are defined in Customizing, determine the allowed receiver for each order type. For example, the standard-settlement receiver control indicator is set in the order if a single settlement of costs to a cost center or CO internal order is desired. The special settlement rule control indicator is set if a distribution rule is used to settle costs to several receivers. In turn, the system automatically generates offsetting entries to the sender objects whereas the debit postings remain in place.

Q-113:   C. Cost settlement receiver

The Controlling component uses orders to plan, monitor and settle operating costs. QM orders are the means by which the activities that are performed during a quality inspection are linked to cost assignment objects in the Controlling component. Like all costs accounted for by the Controlling component, an order category classifies the appraisal costs according to the functional origin of the costs. The functional origin of QM quality costs is indicated by the order category 06. In turn, standard QM order for appraisal costs order types or custom order types are used to collect the costs that originate with inspection activities. To account for appraisal costs using an individual QM order for appraisal costs, the order is created as the inspection lot is created. The order is then assigned to the inspection lot. Following the inspection, inspection activities are recorded in the QM order in terms of activity types that are defined for a work center and related activity times as characteristic inspection results are recorded and valuated or as the usage decision for the inspection lot is documented. The CO component then retrieves predefined prices for the documented activity types and uses the prices to convert the activity times to actual costs. These appraisal costs are settled to a cost object, such as a cost center or a CO internal order, according to a settlement rule that's defined for the QM order master record. In turn, settlement profiles, which are defined in Customizing, determine the allowed receiver for each order type. When the appraisal costs are settled to cost objects, the system generates offsetting entries to the sender objects, whereas the debit postings remain in place.

Q-114:   B. Cost report for a QM order

The Controlling component uses orders to plan, monitor and settle operating costs. QM orders are the means by which the activities that are performed during quality inspections are linked to account assignment objects in the Controlling component. Once the orders are created, the documented appraisal costs data can be evaluated using three different Quality Costs functions: Display QM Orders by Inspection Type, Display Cost Report for QM Order and Display Cost Report for Inspection Lot Confirmed Activities. In particular, the Display Cost Report for QM Order refers to the summarized costs for all materials or inspection lots assigned to a QM order. The report organizes the activity types and costs according to individual cost elements. The user can display the data in the list as a graphic or export the cost data to an Excel spreadsheet. The report can also be printed.

Q-115: A. Plant and B. Inspection type

The Controlling component uses orders to plan, monitor and settle operating costs. QM orders are the means by which the activities that support the processing of quality inspections are linked to account assignment objects in the Controlling component. Like all costs accounted for by the Controlling component, an order category classifies the appraisal costs according to the functional origin of the costs. The functional origin of quality costs is indicated by the order category 06. In turn, standard QM order for appraisal costs order types or custom order types are used to collect the costs that originate with inspection activities. For example, the individual QM order for appraisal costs is a short-term cost collector used to document the actual appraisal costs incurred to process a single inspection lot. Using this order type, activities are selected on the basis of plant, inspection type and/or material and recorded in terms of activity types and activity times in the order. The CO component then retrieves predefined prices for the documented activity types and uses the prices to convert the activity times to actual costs. These inspection costs are settled to cost objects according to account assignments entered when the QM orders were created. In turn, the system automatically generates offsetting entries to the sender objects, whereas the debit postings remain in place.

Q-116: A. Plant

The Controlling component uses orders to plan, monitor and settle operating costs. QM orders are the

means by which the activities that support the processing of quality inspections are linked to account assignment objects in the Controlling component. Like all costs accounted for by the Controlling component, an order category classifies the appraisal costs according to the functional origin of the costs. The functional origin of quality costs is indicated by the order category 06. In turn, standard QM order for appraisal costs order types or custom order types are used to collect the costs that originate with inspection activities. For example, the individual QM order for appraisal costs is a short-term cost collector used to document the actual appraisal costs incurred to process a single inspection lot. Using this order type, activities are selected on the basis of plant, inspection type and/or material and recorded in terms of activity types and activity times in the order. The CO component then retrieves predefined prices for the documented activity types and uses the prices to convert the activity times to actual costs. These inspection costs are settled to cost objects according to account assignments entered when the QM orders were created. In turn, the system automatically generates offsetting entries to the sender objects, whereas the debit postings remain in place.

Q-117: B. Selection of a material from a material class to which the QM order will be assigned

A QM order is assigned to a default class in the Classification System to distinguish one type of quality cost from another and to summarize the quality costs. The class characteristics are used to differentiate the orders. For example, the characteristic origin can be assigned to a class for nonconformity cost orders to differentiate internal nonconformity costs from external nonconformity costs.

Q-118: A. Work center is assigned to cost center and C. Work center is assigned to inspection operation

The Controlling component uses orders to plan, monitor and settle operating costs. QM orders are the means by which the activities that support the processing of quality inspections are linked to account assignment objects in the Controlling component. Like all costs accounted for by the Controlling component, an order category classifies the appraisal costs according to the functional origin of the costs. The functional origin of quality costs is indicated by the order category 06. In turn, standard QM order for appraisal costs order types or custom order types are used to collect the costs that originate with inspection activities. For example, the general QM order for appraisal costs is a long-term cost collector used to collect costs for more than one inspection lot or material and the individual QM order for appraisal costs is a short-term cost collector used to collect inspection costs for a single inspection lot or material. To account for appraisal costs, inspection activities are recorded in QM orders in terms of activity types and activity times as inspection results are recorded or the usage decision for the inspection lot is documented. The CO component then retrieves predefined prices for the documented activity types and uses the prices to convert the activity times to actual costs. These inspection costs are subsequently settled to cost objects, such as a cost center or a CO

233

internal order, according to account assignments entered when the QM orders were created. In turn, the system automatically generates offsetting entries to the sender objects, whereas the debit postings remain in place. The confirmation of activities for quality inspection operations requires the creation of activity types for work centers and activity prices in Controlling, the assignment of work centers to cost objects in PP, the assignment of work centers to plan operations, the definition of standard values for activity types and the assignment of the QM order to the inspection lot in QM.

Q-119:   B. Cost report for QM order

The Controlling component uses orders to plan, monitor and settle operating costs. QM orders are the means by which the activities that are performed during quality inspections are linked to account assignment objects in the Controlling component. Once the orders are created, the documented appraisal costs data can be evaluated using three different Quality Costs functions: Display QM Orders by Inspection Type, Display Cost Report for QM Order and Display Cost Report for Inspection Lot Confirmed Activities. In particular, the Display Cost Report for QM Order refers to the summarized costs for all materials or inspection lots assigned to a QM order. The report organizes the activity types and costs according to individual cost elements. The user can display the data in the list as a graphic or export the cost data to an Excel spreadsheet. The report can also be printed.

Q-120:   A. Define activity types in CO

The Controlling component uses orders to plan, monitor and settle operating costs. QM orders are the means by which the activities that support the processing of quality inspections are linked to account assignment objects in the Controlling component. Like all costs accounted for by the Controlling component, an order category classifies the appraisal costs according to the functional origin of the costs. The functional origin of quality costs is indicated by the order category 06. In turn, standard QM order for appraisal costs order types or custom order types are used to collect the costs that originate with inspection activities. For example, the general QM order for appraisal costs is a long-term cost collector used to collect costs for more than one inspection lot or material. These costs are settled periodically. In turn, the individual QM order for appraisal costs is a short-term cost collector used to collect inspection costs for a single inspection lot or material. These costs are settled on a one-time basis. To account for appraisal costs, inspection activities are recorded in QM orders in terms of activity types and activity times as inspection results are recorded or the usage decision for the inspection lot is documented. The CO component then retrieves predefined prices for the documented activity types and uses the prices to convert the activity times to actual costs. These inspection costs are subsequently settled to cost objects, such as a cost center or a CO internal order, according to account assignments entered when the QM orders were created.   In turn, the system automatically generates offsetting entries to the sender objects,

235

whereas the debit postings remain in place. The confirmation of activities for quality inspection operations requires the creation of activity types for work centers and activity prices in Controlling, the assignment of work centers to cost objects in PP, the assignment of work centers to plan operations, the definition of standard values for activity types and the assignment of the QM order to the inspection lot in QM.

Q-121:   A. Defect costs and D. Warranty costs

Efforts made to assure the quality of a product or service result in quality costs. The functions of the Quality Management component lead to the incurrence of two types of quality costs: appraisal costs and nonconformity costs. Nonconformity costs result from the creation of a product or service, the characteristics of which do not conform to defined specifications or standards. Nonconformity costs include the costs of analyzing product and material defects and the completion of activities, which rectify issues that affect product quality. Such costs include defect costs, rework costs and warranty costs.

Q-122:   B. Cost report for QM order

The Controlling component uses orders to plan, monitor and settle operating costs. QM orders are the means by which the activities that are performed during quality inspections are linked to account assignment objects in the Controlling component. Once the orders are created, the documented appraisal costs data can be

236

evaluated using three different Quality Costs functions: Display QM Orders by Inspection Type, Display Cost Report for QM Order and Display Cost Report for Inspection Lot Confirmed Activities. In particular, the Display Cost Report for QM Order refers to the summarized costs for all materials or inspection lots assigned to a QM order. The report organizes the activity types and costs according to individual cost elements. The user can display the data in the list as a graphic or export the cost data to an Excel spreadsheet. The report can also be printed.

Q-123:   A. Define prices for activity types and C. Assign QM order to inspection lot

The Controlling component uses orders to plan, monitor and settle operating costs. QM orders are the means by which the activities that support the processing of quality inspections are linked to account assignment objects in the Controlling component. Like all costs accounted for by the Controlling component, an order category classifies the appraisal costs according to the functional origin of the costs. The functional origin of quality costs is indicated by the order category 06. In turn, standard QM order for appraisal costs order types or custom order types are used to collect the costs that originate with inspection activities. For example, the general QM order for appraisal costs is a long-term cost collector used to collect costs for more than one inspection lot or material and the individual QM order for appraisal costs is a short-term cost collector used to collect inspection costs for a single inspection lot or material. To account for appraisal costs, inspection activities are recorded in QM orders in terms of activity types and activity times as inspection results are recorded or the usage decision for the inspection lot is documented. The CO component then retrieves predefined prices for the documented activity types and uses the prices to convert the activity times to actual costs. These inspection costs are subsequently settled to cost objects, such as a cost center or a CO internal order, according to account assignments entered when the QM orders were created.   In turn, the system automatically generates offsetting entries to the sender objects, whereas the debit postings remain in place. The confirmation of activities for quality inspection operations requires the creation of activity types for work centers and activity prices in Controlling, the assignment of work centers to cost objects in PP, the assignment of work centers to plan operations, the definition of standard values for activity types and the assignment of the QM order to the inspection lot in QM.

Q-124:   C. CO component

The Controlling component uses orders to plan, monitor and settle operating costs. QM orders are the means by which the activities that support the processing of quality inspections are linked to account assignment objects in the Controlling component. Like all costs accounted for by the Controlling component, an order category classifies the appraisal costs according to the functional origin of the costs. The functional origin of quality costs is indicated by the order category 06. In turn, standard QM order for appraisal costs order types or custom order types are used to collect the costs that originate with inspection activities. For example, the general QM order for appraisal costs is a long-term cost collector used to collect costs for more than one inspection lot or material and the individual QM order for appraisal costs is a short-term cost collector used to collect inspection costs for a single inspection lot or material. To account for appraisal costs, inspection activities are recorded in QM orders in terms of activity types and activity times as inspection results are recorded or the usage decision for the inspection lot is documented. The CO component then retrieves predefined prices for the documented activity types and uses the prices to convert the activity times to actual costs. These inspection costs are subsequently settled to cost objects, such as a cost center or a CO internal order, according to account assignments entered when the QM orders were created. In turn, the system automatically generates offsetting entries to the sender objects, whereas the debit postings remain in place. The confirmation of activities for quality inspection operations requires the creation of activity types for work centers and activity prices in Controlling, the assignment of work centers to cost objects in PP, the assignment of work centers to plan operations, the definition of standard values for activity types and the assignment of the QM order to the inspection lot in QM.

Q-125:   B. Work center is assigned to cost center and C. Work center is assigned to inspection operation

The Controlling component uses orders to plan, monitor and settle operating costs. QM orders are the means by which the activities that support the processing of quality inspections are linked to account assignment objects in the Controlling component. Like all costs accounted for by the Controlling component, an order category classifies the appraisal costs according to the functional origin of the costs. The functional origin of quality costs is indicated by the order category 06. In turn, standard QM order for appraisal costs order types or custom order types are used to collect the costs that originate with inspection activities. To account for appraisal costs, inspection activities are recorded in QM orders in terms of activity types and activity times as inspection results are recorded or the usage decision for the inspection lot is documented. The CO component then retrieves predefined prices for the documented activity types and uses the prices to convert the activity times to actual costs. These inspection costs are subsequently settled to cost objects, such as a cost center or a CO internal order, according to account assignments entered when the QM orders were created. In turn, the system automatically generates offsetting entries to the sender objects, whereas the debit postings remain in place. The confirmation of activities for quality inspection operations requires the creation of activity types for work centers and activity prices in Controlling, the assignment of work centers to cost objects in PP, the assignment of work centers to plan operations, the definition of standard values for activity types and the assignment of the QM order to the inspection lot in QM.

Q-126:   A. Work center is assigned to inspection
operation

The Controlling component uses orders to plan,
monitor and settle operating costs. QM orders are the
means by which the activities that support the
processing of quality inspections are linked to account
assignment objects in the Controlling component. Like
all costs accounted for by the Controlling component,
an order category classifies the appraisal costs according
to the functional origin of the costs. The functional
origin of quality costs is indicated by the order category
06. In turn, standard QM order for appraisal costs
order types or custom order types are used to collect
the costs that originate with inspection activities. To
account for appraisal costs, inspection activities are
recorded in QM orders in terms of activity types and
activity times as inspection results are recorded or the
usage decision for the inspection lot is documented.
The CO component then retrieves predefined prices
for the documented activity types and uses the prices to
convert the activity times to actual costs. These
inspection costs are subsequently settled to cost objects,
such as a cost center or a CO internal order, according
to account assignments entered when the QM orders
were created. In turn, the system automatically
generates offsetting entries to the sender objects,
whereas the debit postings remain in place. The
confirmation of activities for quality inspection
operations requires the creation of activity types for
work centers and activity prices in Controlling, the
assignment of work centers to cost objects in PP, the

241

assignment of work centers to plan operations, the definition of standard values for activity types and the assignment of the QM order to the inspection lot in QM.

Q-127:   C. Incorrect work center is assigned to inspection plan operation

The Controlling component uses orders to plan, monitor and settle operating costs. QM orders are the means by which the activities that support the processing of quality inspections are linked to account assignment objects in the Controlling component. Like all costs accounted for by the Controlling component, an order category classifies the appraisal costs according to the functional origin of the costs. The functional origin of quality costs is indicated by the order category 06. In turn, standard QM order for appraisal costs order types or custom order types are used to collect the costs that originate with inspection activities. To account for appraisal costs, inspection activities are recorded in QM orders in terms of activity types and activity times as inspection results are recorded or the usage decision for the inspection lot is documented. The CO component then retrieves predefined prices for the documented activity types and uses the prices to convert the activity times to actual costs. These inspection costs are subsequently settled to cost objects, such as a cost center or a CO internal order, according to account assignments entered when the QM orders were created. In turn, the system automatically generates offsetting entries to the sender objects, whereas the debit postings remain in place. The confirmation of activities for quality inspection operations requires the creation of activity types for work centers and activity prices in Controlling, the assignment of work centers to cost objects in PP, the assignment of work centers to plan operations, the definition of standard values for activity types and the assignment of the QM order to the inspection lot in QM.

Q-128:   A. Standard settlement receiver control indicator is selected in the QM order

The Controlling component uses orders to plan, monitor and settle operating costs. QM orders are the means by which the activities that are performed during a quality inspection are linked to cost assignment objects in the Controlling component. Like all costs accounted for by the Controlling component, an order category classifies the appraisal costs according to the functional origin of the costs. The functional origin of QM quality costs is indicated by the order category 06. In turn, standard QM order for appraisal costs order types or custom order types are used to collect the costs that originate with inspection activities. Following the inspection, inspection activities are recorded in the QM order in terms of activity types that are defined for a work center and related activity times as characteristic inspection results are recorded and valuated, or as the usage decision for the inspection lot is documented. The CO component then retrieves predefined prices for the documented activity types and uses the prices to convert the activity times to actual costs. These appraisal costs are settled to one or more cost objects, such as a cost center or a CO internal order, according to a settlement rule that's defined for the QM order master record. In turn, settlement profiles, which are defined in Customizing, determine the allowed receiver for each order type. For example, the standard settlement receiver control indicator is set in the order if a single settlement of costs to a cost center or CO internal order is desired. The special settlement rule control indicator is set if a distribution rule is used to settle costs to several receivers. When appraisal costs are settled to cost objects, the system generates offsetting entries to the sender objects, whereas the debit postings remain in place.

Q-129:   B. Cost report for QM order

The Controlling component uses orders to plan, monitor and settle operating costs. QM orders are the means by which the activities that are performed during quality inspections are linked to account assignment objects in the Controlling component. Once the orders are created, the documented appraisal costs data can be evaluated using three different Quality Costs functions: Display QM Orders by Inspection Type, Display Cost Report for QM Order and Display Cost Report for Inspection Lot Confirmed Activities. In particular, the Display Cost Report for QM Order refers to the summarized costs for all materials or inspection lots assigned to a QM order. The report organizes the activity types and costs according to individual cost elements. The user can display the data in the list as a graphic or export the cost data to an Excel spreadsheet. The report can also be printed.

Q-130:   C. Work center and D. Plant

The Controlling component uses orders to plan, monitor and settle operating costs. QM orders are the means by which the activities that are performed during quality inspections are linked to account assignment objects in the Controlling component. The documented appraisal costs data can be evaluated using three different Quality Costs functions: Display QM Orders by Inspection Type, Display Cost Report for QM Order and Display Cost Report for Inspection Lot Confirmed Activities. In particular, the QM Orders by Inspection Type List refers to all materials for which a QM order has been created that meet selection criteria, which includes inspection type, material, plant and QM order. The list, which organizes the orders according to material number, includes material short text, inspection type and inspection type description fields. The user can select an order from the list and display the QM data that's documented in the related material master record or the Controlling data.

Q-131:   D. Costs cannot be assigned to an individual material

The Controlling component uses orders to plan, monitor and settle operating costs. QM orders are the means by which the activities that support the processing of quality inspections are linked to account assignment objects in the Controlling component. Like all costs accounted for by the Controlling component, an order category classifies the appraisal costs according to the functional origin of the costs. The functional origin of quality costs is indicated by the order category 06. In turn, standard QM order for appraisal costs order types or custom order types are used to collect the costs that originate with inspection activities. For example, the general QM order for appraisal costs is a long-term cost collector used to collect costs for more than one inspection lot or material. These costs are settled periodically. In turn, the individual QM order for appraisal costs is a short-term cost collector used to collect inspection costs for a single inspection lot or material. These costs are settled on a one-time basis.

Q-132: B. The CO component converts the activity times to actual costs on the basis of the predefined prices stored in the CO component and C. The CO component identifies the predefined prices associated with the activity types for which the activity times were recorded in the QM component

The Controlling component uses orders to plan, monitor and settle operating costs. QM orders are the means by which the activities that are performed during a quality inspection are linked to cost assignment objects in the Controlling component. Like all costs accounted for by the Controlling component, an order category classifies the appraisal costs according to the functional origin of the costs. The functional origin of QM quality costs is indicated by the order category 06. In turn, standard QM order for appraisal costs order types or custom order types are used to collect the costs that originate with inspection activities. Following an inspection, inspection activities are recorded in the QM order in terms of activity types that are defined for a work center and related activity times as characteristic inspection results are recorded and valuated, or as the usage decision for the inspection lot is documented. The CO component then retrieves predefined prices for the documented activity types and uses the prices to convert the activity times to actual costs. These appraisal costs are settled to one or more cost objects, such as a cost center or a CO internal order. When appraisal costs are settled to cost objects, the system generates offsetting entries to the sender objects, whereas the debit postings remain in place.

Q-133: B. The need exists to assign inspection costs to a particular material or product and D. The need exists to use an automatic function to create the order on an ad hoc basis

The Controlling component uses orders to plan, monitor and settle operating costs. QM orders are the means by which the activities that are performed during a quality inspection are linked to cost assignment objects in the Controlling component. Like all costs accounted for by the Controlling component, an order category classifies the appraisal costs according to the functional origin of the costs. The functional origin of QM quality costs is indicated by the order category 06. In turn, standard QM order for appraisal costs order types or custom order types are used to collect the costs that originate with inspection activities. For example, the individual QM order for appraisal costs is a short-term cost collector used to collect inspection costs for a single inspection lot or material that are settled on a one-time basis. To account for appraisal costs using an individual QM order for appraisal costs, the order is created as the inspection lot is created. The order is then assigned to the inspection lot. Following the inspection, inspection activities are recorded in the QM order in terms of activity types that are defined for a work center and related activity times as characteristic inspection results are recorded and valuated, or as the usage decision for the inspection lot is documented. The CO component then retrieves predefined prices for the documented activity types and uses the prices to convert the activity times to actual costs. These inspection costs are then settled to a cost object, such as a cost center or a CO internal order, according to the settlement rule that's defined for the QM order. In turn, the system automatically generates offsetting entries to the sender object, whereas the debit postings remain in place.

Q-134:   A. Display QM orders by inspection type

The Controlling component uses orders to plan, monitor and settle operating costs. QM orders are the means by which the activities that are performed during quality inspections are linked to account assignment objects in the Controlling component. The documented appraisal costs data can be evaluated using three different Quality Costs functions: Display QM Orders by Inspection Type, Display Cost Report for QM Order and Display Cost Report for Inspection Lot Confirmed Activities. In particular, the QM Orders by Inspection Type List refers to all materials for which a QM order has been created that meet selection criteria, which includes inspection type, material, plant and QM order. The list, which organizes the orders according to material number, includes material short text, inspection type and inspection type description fields. The user can select an order from the list and display the QM data that's documented in the related material master record or the Controlling data.

Q-135:   A. Creation of inspection lot

The Controlling component uses orders to plan, monitor and settle operating costs. QM orders are the means by which the activities that are performed during a quality inspection are linked to account assignment objects in the Controlling component. Like all costs accounted for by the Controlling component, an order category classifies the appraisal costs according to the functional origin of the costs. The functional origin of QM quality costs is indicated by the order category 06. In turn, standard QM order for appraisal costs order types or custom order types are used to collect the costs that originate with inspection activities. The type of QM order used can be determined by the assignment of an order type to the material master record inspection type in Customizing. For example, the general QM order for appraisal costs, QL01, is a long-term cost collector that's created with a manual process and used to collect costs for more than one inspection lot or material. These costs settled periodically. In turn, the individual QM order for appraisal costs, QL02, is a short-term cost collector that's created automatically and used to collect inspection costs for a single inspection lot or material. These costs are settled on a one-time basis. To account for appraisal costs using an individual QM order for appraisal costs, the order is created as the inspection lot is created. The order is then assigned to the inspection lot. Following the inspection, inspection activities are recorded in the QM order in terms of activity types that are defined for a work center and related activity times as characteristic inspection results are recorded and valuated or as the usage decision for the inspection lot is documented. The CO component then retrieves predefined prices for the documented activity types and uses the prices to convert the activity times to actual costs. These inspection costs are then settled to one or more cost objects, such as a cost center or a CO internal order according to the settlement rule that's defined for the QM order. In turn, the system automatically generates offsetting entries to the sender objects, whereas the debit postings remain in place.

Q-136:   A. Complete settlement of costs will occur using a cost center or CO internal order on a one-time basis

The Controlling component uses orders to plan, monitor and settle operating costs. QM orders are the means by which the activities that are performed during a quality inspection are linked to account assignment objects in the Controlling component. Like all costs accounted for by the Controlling component, an order category classifies the appraisal costs according to the functional origin of the costs. The functional origin of QM quality costs is indicated by the order category 06. In turn, standard QM order for appraisal costs order types or custom order types are used to collect the costs

that originate with inspection activities. The type of QM order used can be determined by the assignment of an order type to the material master record inspection type in Customizing. For example, the general QM order for appraisal costs, QL01, is a long-term cost collector that's created with a manual process and used to collect costs for more than one inspection lot or material. These costs settled periodically. In turn, the individual QM order for appraisal costs, QL02, is a short-term cost collector that's created automatically and used to collect inspection costs for a single inspection lot or material. These costs are settled on a one-time basis. To account for appraisal costs using an individual QM order for appraisal costs, the order is created as the inspection lot is created. The order is then assigned to the inspection lot. Following the inspection, inspection activities are recorded in the QM order in terms of activity types that are defined for a work center and related activity times as characteristic inspection results are recorded and valuated or as the usage decision for the inspection lot is documented. The CO component then retrieves predefined prices for the documented activity types and uses the prices to convert the activity times to actual costs. These inspection costs are then settled to one or more cost objects, such as a cost center or a CO internal order according to the settlement rule that's defined for the QM order. In turn, settlement profiles, which are defined in Customizing, determine the allowed receiver for each order type. For example, the standard settlement receiver control indicator is set in the order if a single settlement of costs to a cost center or CO internal order is desired. The special settlement rule control indicator is set if a distribution rule is used to settle costs to several receivers. When appraisal costs are settled to cost objects, the system generates offsetting entries to the sender objects, whereas the debit postings remain in place.

Q-137: B. Plant, D. Inspection type and E. Material class

The Controlling component uses orders to plan, monitor and settle operating costs. QM orders are the means by which the activities that are performed during a quality inspection are linked to account assignment objects in the Controlling component. Like all costs accounted for by the Controlling component, an order category classifies the appraisal costs according to the functional origin of the costs. The functional origin of QM quality costs is indicated by the order category 06. In turn, standard QM order for appraisal costs order types or custom order types are used to collect the costs that originate with inspection activities. The type of QM order used can be determined by the assignment of an order type to the material master record inspection type in Customizing. For example, the general QM order for appraisal costs, QL01, is a long-term cost collector that's created with a manual process and used to collect costs for more than one inspection lot or material. These costs settled periodically. In turn, the individual QM order for appraisal costs, QL02, is a short-term cost collector that's created automatically and used to collect inspection costs for a single inspection lot or material. These costs are settled on a one-time basis. To account for appraisal costs using an individual QM order for appraisal costs, the order is created as the inspection lot is created. The order is then assigned to the inspection lot. Following the inspection, inspection activities are recorded in the QM order in terms of activity types that are defined for a work center and related activity times as characteristic inspection results are recorded and valuated or as the usage decision for the inspection lot is documented. The CO component then retrieves predefined prices for the documented activity types and uses the prices to convert the activity times to actual costs. These inspection costs are then settled to one or more cost objects, such as a cost center or a CO internal order according to the settlement rule that's defined for the QM order. In turn, settlement profiles, which are defined in Customizing, determine the allowed receiver for each order type. For example, the standard settlement receiver control indicator is set in the order if a single settlement of costs to a cost center or CO internal order is desired. The special settlement rule control indicator is set if a distribution rule is used to settle costs to several receivers. When appraisal costs are settled to cost objects, the system generates offsetting entries to the sender objects, whereas the debit postings remain in place.

Q-138:   A. Standard settlement receiver control indicator in the order

The Controlling component uses orders to plan, monitor and settle operating costs. QM orders are the means by which the activities that are performed during a quality inspection are linked to account assignment objects in the Controlling component. Like all costs accounted for by the Controlling component, an order category classifies the appraisal costs according to the functional origin of the costs. The functional origin of QM quality costs is indicated by the order category 06. In turn, standard QM order for appraisal costs order types or custom order types are used to collect the costs that originate with inspection activities. The type of QM order used can be determined by the assignment of an order type to the material master record inspection type in Customizing. For example, the general QM order for appraisal costs, QL01, is a long-term cost collector that's created with a manual process and used to collect costs for more than one inspection lot or material. These costs settled periodically. In turn, the individual QM order for appraisal costs, QL02, is a short-term cost collector that's created automatically and used to collect inspection costs for a single inspection lot or material. These costs are settled on a one-time basis. To account for appraisal costs using an individual QM order for appraisal costs, the order is created as the inspection lot is created. The order is then assigned to the inspection lot. Following the inspection, inspection activities are recorded in the QM order in terms of activity types that are defined for a work center and related activity times as characteristic inspection results are recorded and valuated or as the usage decision for the inspection lot is documented. The CO component then retrieves predefined prices for the documented activity types and uses the prices to convert the activity times to actual costs. These inspection costs are then settled to one or more cost objects, such as a cost center or a CO internal order according to the settlement rule that's defined for the QM order. In turn, settlement profiles, which are defined in Customizing, determine the allowed receiver for each order type. For example, the standard settlement receiver control indicator is set in the order if a single settlement of costs to a cost center or CO internal order is desired. The special settlement rule control indicator is set if a distribution rule is used to settle costs to several receivers. When appraisal costs are settled to cost objects, the system generates offsetting entries to the sender objects, whereas the debit postings remain in place.

Q-139:   A. Incorrect cost center assigned to work center

The Controlling component uses orders to plan, monitor and settle operating costs. QM orders are the means by which the activities that support the processing of quality inspections are linked to account assignment objects in the Controlling component. Like all costs accounted for by the Controlling component, an order category classifies the appraisal costs according to the functional origin of the costs. The functional origin of quality costs is indicated by the order category 06. In turn, standard QM order for appraisal costs order types or custom order types are used to collect the costs that originate with inspection activities. For example, the general QM order for appraisal costs is a long-term cost collector used to collect costs for more than one inspection lot or material and the individual QM order for appraisal costs is a short-term cost collector used to collect inspection costs for a single inspection lot or material. To account for appraisal costs, inspection activities are recorded in QM orders in terms of activity types and activity times as inspection results are recorded or the usage decision for the inspection lot is documented. The CO component then retrieves predefined prices for the documented activity types and uses the prices to convert the activity times to actual costs. These inspection costs are subsequently settled to cost objects, such as a cost center or a CO internal order, according to account assignments entered when the QM orders were created. In turn, the system automatically generates offsetting entries to the sender objects, whereas the debit postings remain in place. The confirmation of activities for quality inspection operations requires the creation of activity types for work centers and activity prices in Controlling, the assignment of work centers to cost objects in PP, the assignment of work centers to plan operations, the definition of standard values for activity types and the assignment of the QM order to the inspection lot in QM.

Q-140:   C. QM

The Controlling component uses orders to plan, monitor and settle operating costs. QM orders are the means by which the activities that support the processing of quality inspections are linked to account assignment objects in the Controlling component. Like all costs accounted for by the Controlling component, an order category classifies the appraisal costs according to the functional origin of the costs. The functional origin of quality costs is indicated by the order category

06. In turn, standard QM order for appraisal costs order types or custom order types are used to collect the costs that originate with inspection activities. To account for appraisal costs, inspection activities are recorded in QM orders in terms of activity types and activity times as inspection results are recorded or the usage decision for the inspection lot is documented. The CO component then retrieves predefined prices for the documented activity types and uses the prices to convert the activity times to actual costs. These inspection costs are subsequently settled to cost objects, such as a cost center or a CO internal order, according to account assignments entered when the QM orders were created. In turn, the system automatically generates offsetting entries to the sender objects, whereas the debit postings remain in place. The confirmation of activities for quality inspection operations requires the creation of activity types for work centers and activity prices in Controlling, the assignment of work centers to cost objects in PP, the assignment of work centers to plan operations, the definition of standard values for activity types and the assignment of the QM order to the inspection lot in QM.

Q-141:   A. CO activities, PP activities, QM activities

The Controlling component uses orders to plan, monitor and settle operating costs. QM orders are the means by which the activities that support the processing of quality inspections are linked to account assignment objects in the Controlling component. Like all costs accounted for by the Controlling component, an order category classifies the appraisal costs according to the functional origin of the costs. The functional origin of quality costs is indicated by the order category 06. In turn, standard QM order for appraisal costs order types or custom order types are used to collect the costs that originate with inspection activities. To account for appraisal costs, inspection activities are recorded in QM orders in terms of activity types and activity times as inspection results are recorded or the usage decision for the inspection lot is documented. The CO component then retrieves predefined prices for the documented activity types and uses the prices to convert the activity times to actual costs. These inspection costs are subsequently settled to cost objects, such as a cost center or a CO internal order, according to account assignments entered when the QM orders were created. In turn, the system automatically generates offsetting entries to the sender objects, whereas the debit postings remain in place. The confirmation of activities for quality inspection operations requires the creation of activity types for work centers and activity prices in Controlling, the assignment of work centers to cost objects in PP, the assignment of work centers to plan operations, the definition of standard values for activity types and the assignment of the QM order to the inspection lot in QM.

Q-142: C. Controlling

The Controlling component uses orders to plan, monitor and settle operating costs. QM orders are the means by which the activities that support the processing of quality inspections are linked to account assignment objects in the Controlling component. Like all costs accounted for by the Controlling component, an order category classifies the appraisal costs according to the functional origin of the costs. The functional origin of quality costs is indicated by the order category 06. In turn, standard QM order for appraisal costs order types or custom order types are used to collect the costs that originate with inspection activities. To account for appraisal costs, inspection activities are recorded in QM orders in terms of activity types and activity times as inspection results are recorded or the usage decision for the inspection lot is documented. The CO component then retrieves predefined prices for the documented activity types and uses the prices to convert the activity times to actual costs. These inspection costs are subsequently settled to cost objects, such as a cost center or a CO internal order, according to account assignments entered when the QM orders were created. In turn, the system automatically generates offsetting entries to the sender objects, whereas the debit postings remain in place. The confirmation of activities for quality inspection operations requires the creation of activity types for work centers and activity prices in Controlling, the assignment of work centers to cost objects in PP, the assignment of work centers to plan operations, the definition of standard values for activity types and the assignment of the QM order to the inspection lot in QM.

Q-143:   B. Work center is assigned to cost center in PP

The Controlling component uses orders to plan, monitor and settle operating costs. QM orders are the means by which the activities that support the processing of quality inspections are linked to account assignment objects in the Controlling component. Like all costs accounted for by the Controlling component, an order category classifies the appraisal costs according to the functional origin of the costs. The functional origin of quality costs is indicated by the order category 06. In turn, standard QM order for appraisal costs order types or custom order types are used to collect the costs that originate with inspection activities. To account for appraisal costs, inspection activities are recorded in QM orders in terms of activity types and activity times as inspection results are recorded or the usage decision for the inspection lot is documented. The CO component then retrieves predefined prices for the documented activity types and uses the prices to convert the activity times to actual costs. These inspection costs are subsequently settled to cost objects, such as a cost center or a CO internal order, according to account assignments entered when the QM orders were created. In turn, the system automatically generates offsetting entries to the sender objects, whereas the debit postings remain in place. The confirmation of activities for quality inspection operations requires the creation of activity types for work centers and activity prices in Controlling, the assignment of work centers to cost objects in PP, the assignment of work centers to plan operations, the definition of standard values for activity types and the assignment of the QM order to the inspection lot in QM.

Q-144:   B. Represented by units of measure including labor hours and C. Represents a group of resources in a cost center

The Controlling component uses orders to plan, monitor and settle operating costs. The QM order is the means by which activities that are performed during a quality inspection are linked to cost accounting objects in the Controlling component. Activities that are performed in the conduct of the quality inspection are recorded in the QM order in terms of activity types that represent a group of resources in cost centers, such as labor hours, and activity times using the QM component. The Controlling component then retrieves the predefined prices for the documented activity types and uses the prices to convert recorded activity times to an actual cost.

Q-145:   A. Quality Notification, B. Quality notification type and E. Account assignment object

The Controlling component uses orders to plan, monitor and settle operating costs. The order is the means by which notification processing activities are linked to cost assignment objects in the Controlling component. Like all costs accounted for by the Controlling component, nonconformity costs are classified according to the functional origin of the costs by means of an order category. The functional origin of quality costs is represented by the order category 06.

In turn, a new or existing QM order for nonconformity costs order type, QN03, is used to collect notification processing costs. Each activity performed to process the notification is recorded in terms of an activity type and activity times. The CO component converts the activity times to an actual cost on the basis of the predefined prices for activity types that are stored in the CO component. The expenses that are incurred to process the notification are then settled to a cost object, such as a cost center or controlling area, according to the account assignment that is entered when the QM order was created. The system automatically generates offsetting entries to the sender objects and the debit postings to the sender object remain in place. The Change Quality Notification function is used to create a QM order for nonconformity costs and assign it to the notification.

Q-146:   B. Appraisal costs and C. Nonconformity costs

Efforts made to assure the quality of a product or service result in quality costs. The functions of the Quality Management component lead to the incurrence of two types of quality costs: appraisal costs and nonconformity costs. Nonconformity costs result from the creation of a product or service, the characteristics of which do not conform to defined specifications or standards. Such costs include defect costs, rework costs and warranty costs. In turn, appraisal costs result from the performance of inspections that confirm the quality of products and the conformance of the products to established benchmarks. Such costs include labor, material and equipment costs.

Q-147:   B. Individual QM order

The Controlling component uses orders to plan, monitor and settle operating costs. QM orders are the means by which the activities that support the processing of quality inspections are linked to account assignment objects in the Controlling component. Like all costs accounted for by the Controlling component, an order category classifies the appraisal costs according to the functional origin of the costs. The functional origin of quality costs is indicated by the order category 06. In turn, the QM order for inspection costs order types are used to collect the costs that originate with inspection activities. For example, the individual QM order for appraisal costs is a short-term cost collector used to collect inspection costs for a single inspection lot or material. After the QM orders are created, inspection activities are recorded in terms of activity types and activity times. The CO component then retrieves predefined prices for the documented activity types and uses the prices to convert the activity times to actual costs. These inspection costs are subsequently settled to cost objects according to account assignments entered when the QM orders were created. In turn, the system automatically generates offsetting entries to the sender objects, whereas the debit postings remain in place.

Q-148:   A. Order type QL01 was used to create the QM order as a cost collector

The Controlling component uses orders to plan, monitor and settle operating costs. QM orders are the means by which the activities that support the processing of quality inspections are linked to account assignment objects in the Controlling component. Like all costs accounted for by the Controlling component, an order category classifies the appraisal costs according to the functional origin of the costs. The functional origin of quality costs is indicated by the order category 06. In turn, standard QM order for appraisal costs order types or custom order types are used to collect the costs that originate with inspection activities. For example, the general QM order for appraisal costs, QL01, is a long-term cost collector used to collect costs for more than one inspection lot or material and the individual QM order for appraisal , QL02, is a short-term cost collector used to collect inspection costs for a single inspection lot or material that's assigned to the order. To account for appraisal costs, inspection activities are recorded in QM orders in terms of activity types and activity times as inspection results are recorded or the usage decision for the inspection lot is documented. The CO component then retrieves predefined prices for the documented activity types and uses the prices to convert the activity times to actual costs. These inspection costs are subsequently settled to cost objects, such as a cost center or a CO internal order, according to account assignments entered when the QM orders were created.   In turn, the system automatically generates offsetting entries to the sender objects, whereas the debit postings remain in place.

Q-149:   A. The CO component uses the price to convert activity times recorded for activity types in QM to actual costs for the activities performed

The Controlling component uses orders to plan, monitor and settle operating costs. QM orders are the means by which the activities that support the processing of quality inspections are linked to account assignment objects in the Controlling component. Like all costs accounted for by the Controlling component, an order category classifies the appraisal costs according to the functional origin of the costs. The functional origin of quality costs is indicated by the order category 06. In turn, the QM order for inspection costs order types or custom order types are used to collect the costs that originate with inspection activities. After the QM orders are created, inspection activities are recorded in terms of activity types and activity times. The CO component then retrieves predefined prices for the documented activity types and uses the prices to convert the activity times to actual costs. These inspection costs are subsequently settled to cost objects according to account assignments entered when the QM orders were created. In turn, the system automatically generates offsetting entries to the sender objects, whereas the debit postings remain in place.

Q-150:   E. None of the above

The Controlling component uses orders to plan, monitor and settle operating costs. QM orders are the means by which the activities that support the processing of quality inspections and notifications are linked to cost assignment objects in the Controlling component. Like all costs accounted for by the Controlling component, Like all costs accounted for by the CO component, appraisal and nonconformity costs are classified according to the functional origin of the costs by means of an order category. The functional origin of quality costs is indicated by the order category 06. In turn, the QM order for inspection costs order types, QL01 and QL02, are used to collect costs that originate with the inspection activities and the QM order type for nonconformity costs, QN03, is used to collect costs that originate with notification-processing activities. A manual process is used to create a QM order for nonconformity costs as the notification is processed.

Q-151:   A. QM order type

The Controlling component uses orders to plan, monitor and settle operating costs. QM orders are the means by which the activities that support the processing of quality inspections and notifications are linked to cost assignment objects in the Controlling component. Like all costs accounted for by the Controlling component, Like all costs accounted for by the CO component, appraisal and nonconformity costs are classified according to the functional origin of the costs by means of an order category. The functional origin of quality costs is indicated by the order category 06. In turn, the QM order for inspection costs order types or custom order types are used to collect costs that originate with the inspection activities. In the case of a QM order for appraisal costs, the order type is assigned to the inspection type in the material master record. This assignment determines the order type to be used to document appraisal costs.

Q-152: A. Post goods movement with account assignment and C. Post goods movement with account assignment to cost center

The Controlling component uses orders to plan, monitor and settle operating costs. QM orders are the means by which the activities that support the processing of quality inspections and notifications are linked to cost assignment objects in the Controlling component. Like all costs accounted for by the Controlling component, Like all costs accounted for by the CO component, appraisal and nonconformity costs are classified according to the functional origin of the costs by means of an order category. The functional origin of quality costs is indicated by the order category 06. In turn, the QM order for inspection costs order types, QL01 and QL02, are used to collect costs that originate with the inspection activities and the QM order type for nonconformity costs, QN03, is used to collect costs that originate with notification-processing activities. A manual process is used to create a QM order for nonconformity costs as the notification is processed. In particular, the order type QL02 is used to post goods movements with account assignments to cost account objects, such as a cost center and CO internal order.

Q-153: B. Special settlement rule control indicator

The Controlling component uses orders to plan, monitor and settle operating costs. QM orders are the means by which the activities that support the processing of quality inspections are linked to account assignment objects in the Controlling component. All costs accounted for by the Controlling component, including appraisal and nonconformity costs, are classified according to the functional origin of the costs. The functional origin of quality costs is indicated by the order category 06, which includes the standard order types QL01, QL02 and QN02. In turn, either the standard QM order types or custom order types are used to collect costs that originate with appraisal and nonconformity activities. For example, the general QM order for appraisal costs is a long-term cost collector used to collect costs for more than one inspection lot or material. In this case, the special settlement receiver control indicator is set in the QM order to ensure the settlement of costs to multiple receivers on the basis of a distribution rule is achieved. In turn, the individual QM order for appraisal costs is a short-term cost collector used to collect inspection costs for a single inspection lot or material. In this case, the standard settlement receiver control indicator is set in the QM order to ensure the settlement of costs to a cost center or internal order.

Q-154:   A. Production order is used as a cost collector for the production inspection type

A number of features distinguish an inspection that is conducted during production. For example, a production inspection is triggered by the creation and release of a production order or process order rather than a QM order.

Q-155:   B. Confirm activities for inspection operations

The Controlling component uses orders to plan, monitor and settle operating costs. QM orders are the means by which the activities that support the processing of quality inspections are linked to account assignment objects in the Controlling component. To account for appraisal costs, inspection activities are recorded in QM orders in terms of activity types and activity times as inspection results are recorded or the usage decision for the inspection lot is documented. The CO component then retrieves predefined prices for the documented activity types and uses the prices to convert the activity times to actual costs. These inspection costs are subsequently settled to cost objects, such as a cost center or a CO internal order, according to account assignments entered when the QM orders were created.   In turn, the system automatically generates offsetting entries to the sender objects, whereas the debit postings remain in place. The confirmation of activities for quality inspection operations requires the creation of activity types for work centers and activity prices in Controlling, the assignment of work centers to cost objects in PP, the assignment of work centers to plan operations, the definition of standard values for activity types and the assignment of the QM order to the inspection lot in QM.

Q-156:   B. Nonconformity costs will be recorded

Efforts made to assure the quality of a product or service result in quality costs. The functions of the Quality Management component lead to the incurrence of two types of quality costs: appraisal costs and nonconformity costs. Nonconformity costs result from the creation of a product or service, the characteristics of which do not conform to defined specifications or standards. Nonconformity costs are incurred as product and material defects are analyzed and activities are performed that rectify the issues that affect product quality. Such issues are documented and addressed by means of notifications. Costs that are incurred as notifications are processed include defect costs, rework costs and warranty expenses.

Q-157:   A. Order category 06

The Controlling component uses orders to plan, monitor and settle operating costs. QM orders are the means by which the activities that support the processing of quality inspections and notifications are linked to cost assignment objects in the Controlling component. Like all costs accounted for by the Controlling component, Like all costs accounted for by the CO component, appraisal and nonconformity costs are classified according to the functional origin of the costs by means of an order category. The functional origin of quality costs is indicated by the order category 06. In turn, the QM order for inspection costs order types, QL01 and QL02, are used to collect costs that originate with the inspection activities and the QM order type for nonconformity costs, QN01, is used to collect costs that originate with notification-processing activities.

Q-158:   A. General QM order for appraisal costs

The Controlling component uses orders to plan, monitor and settle operating costs. QM orders are the means by which the activities that are performed during a quality inspection are linked to account assignment objects in the Controlling component. Like all costs accounted for by the Controlling component, an order category classifies the appraisal costs according to the functional origin of the costs. The functional origin of QM quality costs is indicated by the order category 06. In turn, standard QM order for appraisal costs order types or custom order types are used to collect the costs that originate with inspection activities. The type of QM order used can be determined by the assignment of an order type to the material master record inspection type in Customizing. For example, the general QM order for appraisal costs, QL01, is a long-term cost collector that's created with a manual process and used to collect costs for more than one inspection lot or material. These costs settled periodically. In turn, the individual QM order for appraisal costs, QL02, is a short-term cost collector that's created automatically and used to collect inspection costs for a single inspection lot or material. These costs are settled on a one-time basis.

Q-159:   B. Results Recording and C. Usage Decision

The Controlling component uses orders to plan, monitor and settle operating costs. QM orders are the means by which the activities that support the processing of quality inspections are linked to account assignment objects in the Controlling component. Like all costs accounted for by the Controlling component, an order category classifies the appraisal costs according to the functional origin of the costs. The functional origin of quality costs is indicated by the order category 06. In turn, the QM order for inspection costs order types or custom order types are used to collect the costs that originate with inspection activities. After the QM orders are created, inspection activities are recorded in orders in terms of activity types and activity times. The CO component then retrieves predefined prices for the documented activity types and uses the prices to convert the activity times to actual costs. These inspection costs are subsequently settled to cost objects according to account assignments entered when the QM orders were created. In turn, the system automatically generates offsetting entries to the sender objects, whereas the debit postings remain in place. The Results Recording and Usage Decision functions are used to record activity times that are accounted for by QM orders for appraisal costs.

Q-160:   A. Collect appraisal costs for a material

The Controlling component uses orders to plan, monitor and settle operating costs. QM orders are the means by which the activities that are performed during a quality inspection are linked to account assignment objects in the Controlling component. Like all costs accounted for by the Controlling component, an order category classifies the appraisal costs according to the functional origin of the costs. The functional origin of QM quality costs is indicated by the order category 06. In turn, standard QM order for appraisal costs order types or custom order types are used to collect the costs that originate with inspection activities. The type of QM order used can be determined by the assignment of an order type to the material master record inspection type in Customizing. For example, the general QM order for appraisal costs, QL01, is a long-term cost collector that's created with a manual process and used to collect costs for more than one inspection lot or material. These costs settled periodically. In turn, the individual QM order for appraisal costs, QL02, is a short-term cost collector that's created automatically and used to collect inspection costs for a single inspection lot or material. These costs are settled on a one-time basis. Unlike the QM order type, QL01, the QM order type, QL02 makes it possible to assign the order and appraisal costs directly to an inspection lot.

Q-161:   A. True

The Controlling component uses orders to plan, monitor and settle operating costs. QM orders are the means by which the activities that are performed during a quality inspection are linked to account assignment objects in the Controlling component. Like all costs accounted for by the Controlling component, an order category classifies the appraisal costs according to the functional origin of the costs. The functional origin of QM quality costs is indicated by the order category 06.

In turn, standard QM order for appraisal costs order types or custom order types are used to collect the costs that originate with inspection activities. The type of QM order used can be determined by the assignment of an order type to the material master record inspection type in Customizing. For example, the general QM order for appraisal costs, QL01, is a long-term cost collector that's created with a manual process and used to collect costs for more than one inspection lot or material. These costs settled periodically. In turn, the individual QM order for appraisal costs, QL02, is a short-term cost collector that's created automatically and used to collect inspection costs for a single inspection lot or material. These costs are settled on a one-time basis. Unlike the QM order type, QL01, the QM order type, QL02 makes it possible to assign the order and appraisal costs directly to an inspection lot.

Q-162:   B. Account assignment object for inspection lot

The Controlling component uses orders to plan, monitor and settle operating costs. The QM order is the means by which the costs of activities that are performed during a quality inspection are linked to cost accounting objects in the Controlling component. Activities that are performed in the conduct of the quality inspection are recorded in the QM order in terms of activity types and activity times using the QM component. The Controlling component then retrieves the predefined prices for the documented activity types and uses the prices to convert recorded activity times to an actual cost. The costs are then settled to a cost

274

object according to the account assignment entered
when the QM order was created.

Q-163:   B. Selection criteria for creation of QM orders
by inspection type list

The Controlling component uses orders to plan,
monitor and settle operating costs. QM orders are the
means by which the activities that are performed during
quality inspections are linked to account assignment
objects in the Controlling component. The
documented appraisal costs data can be evaluated using
three different Quality Costs functions: Display QM
Orders by Inspection Type, Display Cost Report for
QM Order and Display Cost Report for Inspection Lot
Confirmed Activities. In particular, the QM Orders by
Inspection Type List refers to all materials for which a
QM order has been created that meet selection criteria,
which includes inspection type, material, plant and QM
order. The list, which organizes the orders according to
material number, includes material short text,
inspection type and inspection type description fields.
The user can select an order from the list and display
the QM data that's documented in the related material
master record or the Controlling data.

Q-164:   B. Assignment of work center to cost center

The Controlling component uses orders to plan,
monitor and settle operating costs. QM orders are the
means by which the activities that support the
processing of quality inspections are linked to account
assignment objects in the Controlling component. To

account for appraisal costs, inspection activities are recorded in QM orders in terms of activity types and activity times as inspection results are recorded or the usage decision for the inspection lot is documented. Next, the CO component retrieves predefined prices for the documented activity types and uses the prices to convert the activity times to actual costs. These inspection costs are subsequently settled to cost objects, such as a cost center or a CO internal order, according to account assignments entered when the QM orders were created. In turn, the system automatically generates offsetting entries to the sender objects, whereas the debit postings remain in place. The confirmation of activities for quality inspection operations requires the creation of activity types for work centers and activity prices in Controlling, the assignment of work centers to cost objects in PP, the assignment of work centers to plan operations, the definition of standard values for activity types and the assignment of the QM order to the inspection lot in QM.

Q-165: A. Inspection operation

The Controlling component uses orders to plan, monitor and settle operating costs. QM orders are the means by which the activities that support the processing of quality inspections are linked to account assignment objects in the Controlling component. To account for appraisal costs, inspection activities are recorded in QM orders in terms of activity types and activity times as inspection results are recorded or the usage decision for the inspection lot is documented.

The confirmation of appraisal activities is performed in reference to an inspection operation. Next, the CO component retrieves predefined prices for the documented activity types and uses the prices to convert the activity times to actual costs. These inspection costs are subsequently settled to cost objects, such as a cost center or a CO internal order, according to account assignments entered when the QM orders were created. In turn, the system automatically generates offsetting entries to the sender objects, whereas the debit postings remain in place.

Q-166:   A. Identify the costs of poor quality and C. Improve productivity

Efforts made to assure the quality of a product or service result in quality costs. The functions of the Quality Management component lead to the incurrence of two types of quality costs: appraisal costs and nonconformity costs. Nonconformity costs result from the creation of a product or service, the characteristics of which do not conform to defined specifications or standards. Such costs include defect costs, rework costs and warranty costs. In turn, appraisal costs result from the performance of inspections that confirm the quality of products and the conformance of the products to established benchmarks. Such costs include labor, material and equipment costs.

Q-167:   D. Controlling

Efforts made to assure the quality of a product or service result in quality costs. The functions of the

Quality Management component lead to the incurrence of two types of quality costs: appraisal costs and nonconformity costs. Nonconformity costs result from the creation of a product or service, the characteristics of which do not conform to defined specifications or standards. Such costs include defect costs, rework costs and warranty costs. In turn, appraisal costs result from the performance of inspections that confirm the quality of products and the conformance of the products to established benchmarks. Such costs include labor, material and equipment costs. The Controlling component uses orders to plan, monitor and settle these operating expenses.

Q-168: A. QM order for appraisal costs for one inspection lot and B. QM order for appraisal costs for more than one inspection lot

The Controlling component uses orders to plan, monitor and settle operating costs. QM orders are the means by which the activities that are performed during a quality inspection are linked to account assignment objects in the Controlling component. Like all costs accounted for by the Controlling component, an order category classifies the appraisal costs according to the functional origin of the costs. The functional origin of QM quality costs is indicated by the order category 06. In turn, standard QM order for appraisal costs order types or custom order types are used to collect the costs that originate with inspection activities. The type of QM order used can be determined by the assignment of an order type to the material master record inspection type in Customizing. For example, the general QM

order for appraisal costs, QL01, is a long-term cost collector that's created with a manual process and used to collect costs for more than one inspection lot or material. These costs settled periodically. In turn, the individual QM order for appraisal costs, QL02, is a short-term cost collector that's created automatically and used to collect inspection costs for a single inspection lot or material. These costs are settled on a one-time basis. Unlike the QM order type, QL01, the QM order type, QL02 makes it possible to assign the order and appraisal costs directly to an inspection lot.

Q-169:   A. Create general QM order for appraisal costs and B. Create individual QM order for appraisal costs

The central maintenance function for QM orders is used to create both general QM orders and individual QM orders for appraisal costs. The function is not used to create a QM order for nonconformity costs. Instead, the Notifications component is used to create the QM order for nonconformity costs.

Q-170:   A. QM order type determined by material master record inspection-type setting, C. QM order type determined by customer enhancement and D. QM order type determined by plant level setting

The Controlling component uses orders to plan, monitor and settle operating costs. QM orders are the means by which the activities that are performed during a quality inspection are linked to account assignment objects in the Controlling component. Like all costs accounted for by the Controlling component, an order category classifies the appraisal costs according to the functional origin of the costs. The functional origin of QM quality costs is indicated by the order category 06. In turn, standard QM order for appraisal costs order types or custom order types are used to collect the costs that originate with inspection activities. The type of QM order used can be determined by the assignment of an order type to the material master record inspection type in Customizing. For example, the general QM order for appraisal costs, QL01, is a long-term cost collector that's created with a manual process and used to collect costs for more than one inspection lot or material. These costs settled periodically. In turn, the individual QM order for appraisal costs, QL02, is a short-term cost collector that's created automatically and used to collect inspection costs for a single inspection lot or material. These costs are settled on a one-time basis. Unlike the QM order type, QL01, the QM order type, QL02 makes it possible to assign the order and appraisal costs directly to an inspection lot. The type of order used to collect appraisal costs is determined by the material master record inspection-type setting, a customer enhancement or a plant-level setting.

Q-171: A. Settlement rules are defined in QM order master records and C. Distribution rule determines how costs are settled

The Controlling component uses orders to plan, monitor and settle operating costs. QM orders are the means by which the activities that are performed during a quality inspection are linked to cost assignment objects in the Controlling component. Like all costs accounted for by the Controlling component, an order category classifies the appraisal costs according to the functional origin of the costs. The functional origin of QM quality costs is indicated by the order category 06. In turn, standard QM order for appraisal costs order types or custom order types are used to collect the costs that originate with inspection activities. Following the inspection, inspection activities are recorded in the QM order in terms of activity types that are defined for a work center and related activity times as characteristic inspection results are recorded and valuated, or as the usage decision for the inspection lot is documented. The CO component then retrieves predefined prices for the documented activity types and uses the prices to convert the activity times to actual costs. These appraisal costs are settled to one or more cost objects, such as a cost center or a CO internal order, according to a settlement rule that's defined for the QM order master record. In turn, settlement profiles, which are defined in Customizing, determine the allowed receiver for each order type. For example, the standard settlement receiver control indicator is set in the order if a single settlement of costs to a cost center or CO internal order is desired. The special settlement rule control indicator is set if a distribution rule is used to settle costs to several receivers. When appraisal costs are settled to cost objects, the system generates offsetting entries to the sender objects, whereas the debit postings remain in place.

Q-172:   A. Change Quality Notification

The Controlling component uses orders to plan, monitor and settle operating costs. QM orders are the means by which the activities that are performed during a quality inspection are linked to account assignment objects in the Controlling component. Like all costs accounted for by the Controlling component, an order category classifies the appraisal costs according to the functional origin of the costs. The functional origin of QM quality costs is indicated by the order category 06. In turn, standard QM order for appraisal costs order types or custom order types are used to collect the costs that originate with inspection activities. The type of QM order used can be determined by the assignment of an order type to the material master record inspection type in Customizing. For example, the general QM order for appraisal costs, QL01, is a long-term cost collector that's created with a manual process and used to collect costs for more than one inspection lot or material. These costs settled periodically. In turn, the individual QM order for appraisal costs, QL02, is a short-term cost collector that's created automatically and used to collect inspection costs for a single inspection lot or material. These costs are settled on a one-time basis. The QM order type for nonconformity costs, QN01, is used to collect costs that originate with notification-processing activities. The Change Quality Notification function is used to create a QM order for nonconformity costs and assign it to the notification.

Q-173: A. QM order is assigned to the quality notification

The Controlling component uses orders to plan, monitor and settle operating costs. QM orders are the means by which the activities that are performed during a quality inspection are linked to account assignment objects in the Controlling component. Like all costs accounted for by the Controlling component, an order category classifies the appraisal costs according to the functional origin of the costs. The functional origin of QM quality costs is indicated by the order category 06. In turn, standard QM order for appraisal costs order types or custom order types are used to collect the costs that originate with inspection activities. The type of QM order used can be determined by the assignment of an order type to the material master record inspection type in Customizing. For example, the general QM order for appraisal costs, QL01, is a long-term cost collector that's created with a manual process and used to collect costs for more than one inspection lot or material. These costs settled periodically. In turn, the individual QM order for appraisal costs, QL02, is a short-term cost collector that's created automatically and used to collect inspection costs for a single inspection lot or material. These costs are settled on a one-time basis. The QM order type for nonconformity costs, QN01, is used to collect costs that originate with notification-processing activities. The Change Quality Notification function is used to create a QM order for nonconformity costs and assign it to the notification. The Change Quality Notification function is used to create a QM order for nonconformity costs and assign it to the notification.

Q-174:   C. Special settlement rule

The Controlling component uses orders to plan, monitor and settle operating costs. QM orders are the means by which the activities that are performed during a quality inspection are linked to cost assignment objects in the Controlling component. Like all costs accounted for by the Controlling component, an order category classifies the appraisal costs according to the functional origin of the costs. The functional origin of QM quality costs is indicated by the order category 06. In turn, standard QM order for appraisal costs order types or custom order types are used to collect the costs that originate with inspection activities. Following the inspection, inspection activities are recorded in the QM order in terms of activity types that are defined for a work center and related activity times as characteristic inspection results are recorded and valuated, or as the usage decision for the inspection lot is documented. The CO component then retrieves predefined prices for the documented activity types and uses the prices to convert the activity times to actual costs. These appraisal costs are settled to one or more cost objects, such as a cost center or a CO internal order, according to a settlement rule that's defined for the QM order master record. In turn, settlement profiles, which are defined in Customizing, determine the allowed receiver for each order type. For example, the standard settlement receiver control indicator is set in the order if a single settlement of costs to a cost center or CO internal order is desired. The special settlement rule control indicator is set if a distribution rule is used to settle costs to several receivers. When appraisal costs are settled to cost objects, the system generates offsetting entries to the sender objects, whereas the debit postings remain in place.

Q-175:   C. Standard settlement receiver

The Controlling component uses orders to plan, monitor and settle operating costs. QM orders are the means by which the activities that are performed during a quality inspection are linked to cost assignment objects in the Controlling component. Like all costs accounted for by the Controlling component, an order category classifies the appraisal costs according to the functional origin of the costs. The functional origin of QM quality costs is indicated by the order category 06. In turn, standard QM order for appraisal costs order types or custom order types are used to collect the costs that originate with inspection activities. Following the inspection, inspection activities are recorded in the QM order in terms of activity types that are defined for a work center and related activity times as characteristic inspection results are recorded and valuated, or as the usage decision for the inspection lot is documented. The CO component then retrieves predefined prices for the documented activity types and uses the prices to convert the activity times to actual costs. These appraisal costs are settled to one or more cost objects, such as a cost center or a CO internal order, according to a settlement rule that's defined for the QM order master record. In turn, settlement profiles, which are defined in Customizing, determine the allowed receiver for each order type. For example, the standard settlement receiver control indicator is set in the order if a single settlement of costs to a cost center or CO internal order is desired. The special settlement rule control indicator is set if a distribution rule is used to settle costs to several receivers. When appraisal costs are settled to cost objects, the system generates offsetting entries to the sender objects, whereas the debit postings remain in place.

Q-176:   B. Standard settlement rule is selected

The Controlling component uses orders to plan, monitor and settle operating costs. QM orders are the means by which the activities that are performed during a quality inspection are linked to cost assignment objects in the Controlling component. Like all costs accounted for by the Controlling component, an order category classifies the appraisal costs according to the functional origin of the costs. The functional origin of QM quality costs is indicated by the order category 06. In turn, standard QM order for appraisal costs order types or custom order types are used to collect the costs that originate with inspection activities. Following the inspection, inspection activities are recorded in the QM order in terms of activity types that are defined for a work center and related activity times as characteristic inspection results are recorded and valuated, or as the usage decision for the inspection lot is documented. The CO component then retrieves predefined prices for the documented activity types and uses the prices to convert the activity times to actual costs. These appraisal costs are settled to one or more cost objects, such as a cost center or a CO internal order, according to a settlement rule that's defined for the QM order master record. In turn, settlement profiles, which are defined in Customizing, determine the allowed receiver for each order type. For example, the standard settlement receiver control indicator is set in the order if a single settlement of costs to a cost center or CO internal order is desired. The special settlement rule control indicator is set if a distribution rule is used to settle costs to several receivers. When appraisal costs are settled to cost objects, the system generates offsetting entries to the sender objects, whereas the debit postings remain in place.

Q-177:   D. All of the above

The Controlling component uses orders to plan, monitor and settle operating costs. QM orders are the means by which the activities that support the processing of quality inspections are linked to account assignment objects in the Controlling component. Like all costs accounted for by the Controlling component, an order category classifies the appraisal costs according to the functional origin of the costs. The functional origin of quality costs is indicated by the order category 06. In turn, standard QM order for appraisal costs order types or custom order types are used to collect the costs that originate with inspection activities. To account for appraisal costs, inspection activities are recorded in QM orders in terms of activity types and activity times as inspection results are recorded or the usage decision for the inspection lot is documented. The CO component then retrieves predefined prices for the documented activity types and uses the prices to convert the activity times to actual costs. These inspection costs are subsequently settled to cost objects, such as a cost center or a CO internal order, according to account assignments entered when the QM orders were created. The confirmation of activities for quality inspection operations requires the creation of activity types for work centers and activity prices in Controlling, the assignment of work centers to cost objects in PP, the assignment of work centers to plan operations, the definition of standard values for activity types and the assignment of the QM order to the inspection lot in QM. If incorrect values are recorded as appraisal costs are settled, the activity type prices, the activities defined for a work center and the assignment of the work center to the inspection plan operation should be checked.

Q-178:   D. All of the above

The Controlling component uses orders to plan, monitor and settle operating costs. QM orders are the means by which the activities that support the processing of quality inspections are linked to account assignment objects in the Controlling component. To account for appraisal costs, inspection activities are recorded in QM orders in terms of activity types and activity times as inspection results are recorded or the usage decision for the inspection lot is documented. The CO component then retrieves predefined prices for the documented activity types and uses the prices to convert the activity times to actual costs. These inspection costs are subsequently settled to cost objects, such as a cost center or a CO internal order, according to account assignments entered when the QM orders were created.   In turn, the system automatically generates offsetting entries to the sender objects, whereas the debit postings remain in place. The confirmation of activities for quality inspection operations requires the creation of activity types for work centers and activity prices in Controlling, the assignment of work centers to cost objects in PP, the assignment of work centers to plan operations, the definition of standard values for activity types and the assignment of the QM order to the inspection lot in QM.

Q-179:   B. Prerequisites to the confirmation of activities for an inspection operation

The Controlling component uses orders to plan, monitor and settle operating costs. QM orders are the means by which the activities that support the processing of quality inspections are linked to account assignment objects in the Controlling component. To account for appraisal costs, inspection activities are recorded in QM orders in terms of activity types and activity times as inspection results are recorded or the usage decision for the inspection lot is documented. The CO component then retrieves predefined prices for the documented activity types and uses the prices to convert the activity times to actual costs. These inspection costs are subsequently settled to cost objects, such as a cost center or a CO internal order, according to account assignments entered when the QM orders were created.   In turn, the system automatically generates offsetting entries to the sender objects, whereas the debit postings remain in place. The confirmation of activities for quality inspection operations requires the creation of activity types for work centers and activity prices in Controlling, the assignment of work centers to cost objects in PP, the assignment of work centers to plan operations, the definition of standard values for activity types and the assignment of the QM order to the inspection lot in QM.

Q-180:   D. Work center and E. Plant

The Controlling component uses orders to plan, monitor and settle operating costs. QM orders are the means by which the activities that support the processing of quality inspections are linked to account assignment objects in the Controlling component. To account for appraisal costs, inspection activities are recorded in QM orders in terms of activity types and activity times as inspection results are recorded or the usage decision for the inspection lot is documented. The CO component then retrieves predefined prices for the documented activity types and uses the prices to convert the activity times to actual costs. These inspection costs are subsequently settled to cost objects, such as a cost center or a CO internal order, according to account assignments entered when the QM orders were created.   In turn, the system automatically generates offsetting entries to the sender objects, whereas the debit postings remain in place. The confirmation of activities for quality inspection operations requires the creation of activity types for work centers and activity prices in Controlling, the assignment of work centers to cost objects in PP, the assignment of work centers to plan operations, the definition of standard values for activity types and the assignment of the QM order to the inspection lot in QM.

Q-181:   A. Custom QM order type and D. Individual QM order for appraisal costs

The Controlling component uses orders to plan, monitor and settle operating costs. QM orders are the means by which the activities that are performed during a quality inspection are linked to account assignment objects in the Controlling component. Like all costs accounted for by the Controlling component, an order category classifies the appraisal costs according to the functional origin of the costs. The functional origin of QM quality costs is indicated by the order category 06. In turn, standard QM order for appraisal costs order types or custom order types are used to collect the costs that originate with inspection activities. The type of QM order used can be determined by the assignment of an order type to the material master record inspection type in Customizing.   For example, the general QM order for appraisal costs, QL01, is a long-term cost collector that's created with a manual process and used to collect costs for more than one inspection lot or material. These costs settled periodically. In turn, the individual QM order for appraisal costs, QL02, is a short-term cost collector that's created automatically and used to collect inspection costs for a single inspection lot or material. These costs are settled on a one-time basis. The QM order type for nonconformity costs, QN01, is used to collect costs that originate with notification-processing activities. Custom order types can also be used.

Q-182: A. Documents costs that originate with inspection activities

Efforts made to assure the quality of a product or service result in quality costs. The functions of the Quality Management component lead to the incurrence of two types of quality costs: appraisal costs and nonconformity costs. Nonconformity costs result from the creation of a product or service, the characteristics of which do not conform to defined specifications or standards. Such costs include defect costs, rework costs and warranty costs. In turn, appraisal costs result from the performance of inspections that confirm the quality of products and the conformance of the products to established benchmarks. Such costs include labor, material and equipment costs. The Controlling component uses orders to plan, monitor and settle these operating expenses.

Q-183: B. Plant

The Controlling component uses orders to plan, monitor and settle operating costs. QM orders are the means by which the activities that support the processing of quality inspections are linked to account assignment objects in the Controlling component. If the central maintenance function is used to create and assign a QM order, required entries include plant, inspection type, and/or material and cost object.

Q-184:   A. Material costs, C. Labor costs and D. Equipment costs

Efforts made to assure the quality of a product or service result in quality costs. The functions of the Quality Management component lead to the incurrence of two types of quality costs: appraisal costs and nonconformity costs. Nonconformity costs result from the creation of a product or service, the characteristics of which do not conform to defined specifications or standards. Such costs include defect costs, rework costs and warranty costs. In turn, appraisal costs result from the performance of inspections that confirm the quality of products and the conformance of the products to established benchmarks. Such costs include labor, material and equipment costs. The Controlling component uses orders to plan, monitor and settle these operating expenses.

Q-185:   A. Collect costs that arise due to the poor quality of goods

The Controlling component uses orders to plan, monitor and settle operating costs. QM orders are the means by which the activities that are performed during a quality inspection are linked to account assignment objects in the Controlling component. Like all costs accounted for by the Controlling component, an order category classifies the appraisal costs according to the functional origin of the costs. The functional origin of QM quality costs is indicated by the order category 06. In turn, standard QM order for appraisal costs order types or custom order types are used to collect the costs

that originate with inspection activities. The type of QM order used can be determined by the assignment of an order type to the material master record inspection type in Customizing. For example, the general QM order for appraisal costs, QL01, is a long-term cost collector that's created with a manual process and used to collect costs for more than one inspection lot or material. These costs settled periodically. In turn, the individual QM order for appraisal costs, QL02, is a short-term cost collector that's created automatically and used to collect inspection costs for a single inspection lot or material. These costs are settled on a one-time basis. The QM order type for nonconformity costs, QN01, is used to collect costs that originate with notification-processing activities. Custom order types can also be used.

Q-186:   A. Long-term cost collector and D. Cost collector for more than one material or inspection lot

The Controlling component uses orders to plan, monitor and settle operating costs. QM orders are the means by which the activities that are performed during a quality inspection are linked to account assignment objects in the Controlling component. Like all costs accounted for by the Controlling component, an order category classifies the appraisal costs according to the functional origin of the costs. The functional origin of QM quality costs is indicated by the order category 06. In turn, standard QM order for appraisal costs order types or custom order types are used to collect the costs that originate with inspection activities. The type of QM order used can be determined by the assignment of an order type to the material master record inspection type in Customizing. For example, the general QM order for appraisal costs, QL01, is a long-term cost collector that's created with a manual process and used to collect costs for more than one inspection lot or material. These costs settled periodically. In turn, the individual QM order for appraisal costs, QL02, is a short-term cost collector that's created automatically and used to collect inspection costs for a single inspection lot or material. These costs are settled on a one-time basis. The QM order type for nonconformity costs, QN01, is used to collect costs that originate with notification-processing activities. Custom order types can also be used.

Q-187:   C. CO

The Controlling component uses orders to plan, monitor and settle operating costs. QM orders are the means by which the activities that are performed during a quality inspection are linked to cost assignment objects in the Controlling component. Like all costs accounted for by the Controlling component, an order category classifies the appraisal costs according to the functional origin of the costs. The functional origin of QM quality costs is indicated by the order category 06. In turn, standard QM order for appraisal costs order types or custom order types are used to collect the costs that originate with inspection activities. Following the inspection, inspection activities are recorded in the QM order in terms of activity types that are defined for a work center and related activity times as characteristic inspection results are recorded and valuated, or as the usage decision for the inspection lot is documented. Next, the CO component retrieves predefined prices for the documented activity types and uses the prices to convert the activity times to actual costs. These appraisal costs are settled to one or more cost objects, such as a cost center or a CO internal order, according to a settlement rule that's defined for the QM order master record. In turn, settlement profiles, which are defined in Customizing, determine the allowed receiver for each order type. When appraisal costs are settled to cost objects, the system generates offsetting entries to the sender objects, whereas the debit postings remain in place.

Q-188:   B. QL02 and C. QN01

The Controlling component uses orders to plan, monitor and settle operating costs. QM orders are the means by which the activities that are performed during a quality inspection are linked to account assignment objects in the Controlling component. Like all costs accounted for by the Controlling component, an order category classifies the appraisal costs according to the functional origin of the costs. The functional origin of QM quality costs is indicated by the order category 06. In turn, standard QM order for appraisal costs order types or custom order types are used to collect the costs that originate with inspection activities. The type of QM order used can be determined by the assignment of an order type to the material master record inspection type in Customizing. For example, the general QM order for appraisal costs, QL01, is a long-term cost collector that's created with a manual process and used to collect costs for more than one inspection lot or material. These costs settled periodically. In turn, the individual QM order for appraisal costs, QL02, is a short-term cost collector that's created automatically and used to collect inspection costs for a single inspection lot or material. These costs are settled on a one-time basis. The QM order type for nonconformity costs, QN01, is used to collect costs that originate with notification-processing activities. Custom order types can also be used.

Q-189:   A. Order is assigned to the notification header and B. The costs for the order are settled in the Controlling component

The Controlling component uses orders to plan, monitor and settle operating costs. The order, which is assigned to the notification header, is the means by which activities that support the processing of quality notifications are linked to cost assignment objects in the Controlling component. Like all costs accounted for by the Controlling component, nonconformity costs are classified according to the functional origin of the costs by means of an order category. The functional origin of quality costs is indicated by the order category 06. In turn, the QM order for nonconformity costs order type, QN03, is created manually and used to collect costs that originate with the activities that are performed as the notification is processed. Each activity is recorded in terms of an activity type and activity times. The CO component then identifies the predefined prices associated with the activity types for which the activity times were recorded in QM. The CO component converts the activity times to an actual cost on the basis of the predefined prices stored in the CO component. The expenses that are incurred to process the notification are then settled to a cost object, such as a cost center or controlling area, according to the account assignment that is entered when the QM order was created. During settlement, all of the actual costs incurred to process the notification are allocated to one or more receivers. The system then automatically generates offsetting entries to the sender objects and the debit postings to the sender objects remain in place.

Q-190:   A. Cost center and B. CO internal order

The Controlling component uses orders to plan, monitor and settle operating costs. QM orders are the means by which the activities that support the processing of quality inspections are linked to account assignment objects in the Controlling component. Like all costs accounted for by the Controlling component, an order category classifies the appraisal costs according to the functional origin of the costs. The functional origin of quality costs is indicated by the order category 06. In turn, standard QM order for appraisal costs order types or custom order types are used to collect the costs that originate with inspection activities.   To account for appraisal costs, inspection activities are recorded in QM orders in terms of activity types and activity times as inspection results are recorded or the usage decision for the inspection lot is documented. The CO component then retrieves predefined prices for the documented activity types and uses the prices to convert the activity times to actual costs. These inspection costs are subsequently settled to cost objects, such as a cost center or a CO internal order, according to account assignments entered when the QM orders were created. In turn, the system generates offsetting entries to the sender objects and the debit postings remain in place.

Q-191: A. Maintain Material Master Record and C. Central Maintenance

The Controlling component uses orders to plan, monitor and settle operating costs. QM orders are the means by which the activities that support the processing of quality inspections are linked to account assignment objects in the Controlling component. Like all costs accounted for by the Controlling component, an order category classifies the appraisal costs according to the functional origin of the costs. The functional origin of quality costs is indicated by the order category 06. In turn, the individual QM order for inspection costs order type is used to collect costs that originate with the activities that are performed as an inspection is processed. In the event of an individual QM order for appraisal costs, the order type is assigned to the inspection type in the Material Master record. This assignment determines the order type to be used to document appraisal costs. Both the Maintain Material Master function and the Central Maintenance function for QM order can be used to create and assign a QM order to a material master record.

Q-192: A. QM order

The Controlling component uses orders to plan, monitor and settle operating costs. QM orders are the means by which the activities that support the processing of quality inspections are linked to account assignment objects in the Controlling component. Like all costs accounted for by the Controlling component, an order category classifies the appraisal costs according to the functional origin of the costs. The functional origin of quality costs is indicated by the order category 06. In turn, standard QM order for appraisal costs order types or custom order types are used to collect the costs that originate with inspection activities. For example, the general QM order for appraisal costs is a long-term cost collector used to collect costs for more than one inspection lot or material. In this case, the special settlement receiver control indicator is set in the QM order to ensure the settlement of costs to multiple receivers or an account assignment object on the basis of a distribution rule is achieved. In turn, the individual QM order for appraisal costs is a short-term cost collector used to collect inspection costs for a single inspection lot or material. In this case, the standard settlement receiver control indicator is set in the QM order to ensure the settlement of costs to a cost center or internal order

Q-193: C. The need does exist to settle the accumulated costs on an as incurred basis and D. The need does exist to use an automatic function to create the order

The Controlling component uses orders to plan, monitor and settle operating costs. QM orders are the

means by which the activities that support the processing of quality inspections are linked to account assignment objects in the Controlling component. Like all costs accounted for by the Controlling component, an order category classifies the appraisal costs according to the functional origin of the costs. The functional origin of quality costs is indicated by the order category 06. In turn, standard QM order for appraisal costs order types or custom order types are used to collect the costs that originate with inspection activities. For example, the general QM order for appraisal costs is a long-term cost collector used to collect costs for more than one inspection lot or material. In this case, the special settlement receiver control indicator is set in the QM order to ensure the settlement of costs to multiple receivers or an account assignment object on the basis of a distribution rule is achieved. In turn, the individual QM order for appraisal costs is a short-term cost collector used to collect inspection costs for a single inspection lot or material. In this case, the standard settlement receiver control indicator is set in the QM order to ensure the settlement of costs to a cost center or internal order.

Q-194:   A. Settlement of costs to a single cost center or CO internal order

The Controlling component uses orders to plan, monitor and settle operating costs. QM orders are the means by which the activities that support the processing of quality inspections are linked to account assignment objects in the Controlling component. Like all costs accounted for by the Controlling component, an order category classifies the appraisal costs according to the functional origin of the costs. The functional origin of quality costs is indicated by the order category 06. In turn, standard QM order for appraisal costs order types or custom order types are used to collect the costs that originate with inspection activities. For example, the general QM order for appraisal costs is a long-term cost collector used to collect costs for more than one inspection lot or material. In this case, the special settlement receiver control indicator is set in the QM order to ensure the settlement of costs to multiple receivers or an account assignment object on the basis of a distribution rule is achieved. In turn, the individual QM order for appraisal costs is a short-term cost collector used to collect inspection costs for a single inspection lot or material. In this case, the standard settlement receiver control indicator is set in the QM order to ensure the settlement of costs to a cost center or internal order.

Q-195:   B. Rework costs will be understated and D. Warranty costs will be understated

Efforts to assure the quality of a product or service result in quality costs. The functions of the Quality Management component lead to the incurrence of two types of quality costs: appraisal costs and nonconformity costs. Nonconformity costs result from the creation of a product or service, the characteristics of which do not conform to defined specifications or standards. Such costs include defect costs, rework costs and warranty costs. If nonconformity costs are not settled to cost objects when the notification is completed, the actual nonconformity costs, such as rework costs and warranty costs, will be understated.

Q-196:   A. Inspection settings in material master record

The Controlling component uses orders to plan, monitor and settle operating costs. QM orders are the means by which the activities that are performed during a quality inspection are linked to account assignment objects in the Controlling component. Like all costs accounted for by the Controlling component, an order category classifies the appraisal costs according to the functional origin of the costs. The functional origin of QM quality costs is indicated by the order category 06. In turn, standard QM order for appraisal costs order types or custom order types are used to collect the costs that originate with inspection activities. The type of QM order used can be determined by the assignment of an order type to the material master record inspection type in Customizing.   For example, the general QM order for appraisal costs, QL01, is a long-term cost collector that's created with a manual process and used to collect costs for more than one inspection lot or material. These costs settled periodically. In turn, the individual QM order for appraisal costs, QL02, is a short-term cost collector that's created automatically and used to collect inspection costs for a single inspection lot or material. These costs are settled on a one-time basis. To control the QM order type used to document appraisal costs, the order type is assigned to the inspection type in the Material Master record.

Q-197:   A. Assign work center to cost center

The Controlling component uses orders to plan, monitor and settle operating costs. QM orders are the means by which the activities that support the processing of quality inspections are linked to account assignment objects in the Controlling component. Standard QM order for appraisal costs order types or custom order types are used to collect the costs that originate with inspection activities. To account for appraisal costs, inspection activities are recorded in QM orders in terms of activity types and activity times as inspection results are recorded or the usage decision for the inspection lot is documented. The CO component retrieves predefined prices for the documented activity types and uses the prices to convert the activity times to actual costs. These inspection costs are subsequently settled to cost objects according to account assignments entered when the QM orders were created. In turn, the system automatically generates offsetting entries to the sender objects, whereas the debit postings remain in place. The confirmation of activities for quality inspection operations requires the creation of activity types for work centers and activity prices in Controlling, the assignment of work centers to cost objects in PP, the assignment of work centers to plan operations, the definition of standard values for activity types and the assignment of the QM order to the inspection lot in QM.

Q-198:   A. Results Recording and C. Usage Decision

The Controlling component uses orders to plan, monitor and settle operating costs. QM orders are the means by which the activities that support the processing of quality inspections are linked to account assignment objects in the Controlling component. Standard QM order for appraisal costs order types or custom order types are used to collect the costs that originate with inspection activities. To account for appraisal costs, inspection activities are recorded in QM orders in terms of activity types and activity times as inspection results are recorded or the usage decision for the inspection lot is documented. The CO component retrieves predefined prices for the documented activity types and uses the prices to convert the activity times to actual costs. These inspection costs are subsequently settled to cost objects according to account assignments entered when the QM orders were created. In turn, the system automatically generates offsetting entries to the sender objects, whereas the debit postings remain in place. The Results Recording and Usage Decision functions are used to record activity times that are accounted for by a general QM order for appraisal costs.

Q-199:   A. Activity times must be recorded for a QM order

The Controlling component uses orders to plan, monitor and settle operating costs. QM orders are the means by which the activities that support the processing of quality inspections are linked to account assignment objects in the Controlling component. Standard QM order for appraisal costs order types or custom order types are used to collect the costs that originate with inspection activities. To account for appraisal costs, inspection activities are recorded in QM orders in terms of activity types and activity times as inspection results are recorded or the usage decision for the inspection lot is documented. The CO component retrieves predefined prices for the documented activity types and uses the prices to convert the activity times to actual costs. These inspection costs are subsequently settled to cost objects according to account assignments entered when the QM orders were created. In turn, the system automatically generates offsetting entries to the sender objects, whereas the debit postings remain in place. If the milestone confirmation or confirmation required control key is set for an inspection operation, recording activity times is a mandatory process.

Q-200:   B. Assignment of work center to cost center in PP and C. Prices defined for activity types in CO

The Controlling component uses orders to plan, monitor and settle operating costs. QM orders are the means by which the activities that support the processing of quality inspections are linked to account assignment objects in the Controlling component. Standard QM order for appraisal costs order types or custom order types are used to collect the costs that originate with inspection activities. To account for appraisal costs, inspection activities are recorded in QM orders in terms of activity types and activity times as inspection results are recorded or the usage decision for the inspection lot is documented. The CO component retrieves predefined prices for the documented activity types and uses the prices to convert the activity times to actual costs. These inspection costs are subsequently settled to cost objects according to account assignments entered when the QM orders were created. In turn, the system automatically generates offsetting entries to the sender objects, whereas the debit postings remain in place. The confirmation of activities for quality inspection operations requires the creation of activity types for work centers and activity prices in Controlling, the assignment of work centers to cost objects in PP, the assignment of work centers to plan operations, the definition of standard values for activity types and the assignment of the QM order to the inspection lot in QM.

Q-201:   A. Special settlement receiver

The Controlling component uses orders to plan, monitor and settle operating costs. QM orders are the means by which the activities that support the processing of quality inspections are linked to account assignment objects in the Controlling component. Like all costs accounted for by the Controlling component, an order category classifies the appraisal costs according to the functional origin of the costs. The functional origin of quality costs is indicated by the order category 06. In turn, standard QM order for appraisal costs order types or custom order types are used to collect the costs that originate with inspection activities. For example, the general QM order for appraisal costs is a long-term cost collector used to collect costs for more than one inspection lot or material. In this case, the special settlement receiver control indicator is set in the

QM order to ensure the settlement of costs to multiple receivers or an account assignment object on the basis of a distribution rule is achieved. In turn, the individual QM order for appraisal costs is a short-term cost collector used to collect inspection costs for a single inspection lot or material. In this case, the standard settlement receiver control indicator is set in the QM order to ensure the settlement of costs to a cost center or internal order.

www.ingramcontent.com/pod-product-compliance
Lightning Source LLC
Chambersburg PA
CBHW070934050326
40689CB00014B/3204